Parker County Legends

Trail Bosses and Wild Hosses

Dedication
This book is dedicated in Honor and Memory
Of
Ikard Smith
1919-2006

He was the inspiration for this book.

Parker County Legends
Trail Bosses Wild Hosses

The ***true and factual stories*** of three great cowboys who were used for
the fictional back up of the *Lonesome Dove* book and movie
Charles Goodnight, Oliver Loving and Bose Ikard
~All had connections to Weatherford and Parker County, Texas~

Charles Goodnight and Oliver Loving were both "white"
and Bose Ikard was "black." What a great team of cowboys.

This book is the fourth book of Parker County history published by

Nebo Valley Press
Leon Tanner and Mary Kemp
2603 S. Main St.
Weatherford, Texas

Proceeds from this book will benefit
The Abandoned Cemetery Association of Parker County, Inc.
and other local charities.

Bar Code: BNO 9726133-2-3

The Book Makers

Acknowledgements with THANKS to all:

First, thanks to Judy James and Pam Tarpley for the complete stories in Section II, Oliver Loving, and Section III, Charles Goodnight. They did a great job and also helped us (Mary Kemp and Leon Tanner) with our computers and did some great publicity on Judy James's weekly Saturday radio program.

****

Next, let's thank Sarah Slee Anderson, who came in at the last minute to help us with our Section IV, Bose Ikard. She was the former editor of the *Weatherford Democrat* and has helped us many times in the past.

****

It is great to have next door neighbors who help even at the last minute – when your computer breaks down. Thanks Lois Johnson for winding things up.

****

Thanks for the great cover design prepared by:

Photo Design Photography
Les and Cecilia Lopez
Coronado Ct. Weatherford, Texas

Long time friends who do great work

****

Last but not least. Thanks to Jay Love of:

Taylor Publishing, Co.
1550 West Mockingbird Lane
Dallas, Texas

For not only printing this, our third book,
but for also being such a great friend and advisor.

****

And to Leon Tanner: Thank you for letting me (Mary) do things my way (sometimes) and getting on with planning the next book about Brigadier General Lecil Lee, one of the greatest generals of any war, and who was born and raised on the eastside of Weatherford, Texas, where the Tanner family settled in 1890.

Introduction
By: Mary Kemp

After much thought concerning this opening introduction article, I have come up with mixed emotions. Actually, I feel the lives of these three Parker County Cowboys have been written about so much that they need no introduction. Yet every day something new is reported. So, we hope you will find something extra in this book full of the legends of such famous cowboys.

Now we all know about the famous book and movie, *"Lonesome Dove"*, as offered by Larry McMurtry. You might find it interesting to know how I became involved with the book and movie which is well documented and "fiction".

So here we go. About the time the book, *"Lonesome Dove"* was published, I was working to obtain three Texas Historical Markers for the Parker County Historical Commission. They were for J.R. Couts, G.A. Holland and Bose Ikard. At the time I considered the first two gentlemen to be of the most historical importance, but I also knew that Bose was more of a cowboy legend where the other two were historical and famous for other reasons. All three of the markers were dedicated on October 14, 1990. Great crowds attended the ceremonies the same afternoon, but the Bose Ikard crowd was something else in size with many out of town dignitaries attending. Why? Well I actually knew but was a little hesitant to expand on the subject at this time.

You see, sometime after the *"Lonesome Dove"* book was published in 1985, I had a visitor in my Texas Butane Company office located on the South side of the Court House square in Weatherford. A very nice man entered and asked for directions to the graves of Loving and Ikard. After I gave him directions, he said he was Larry McMurtry and had I read the book he had written entitled *"Lonesome Dove"*. Of course I had not even heard of it but said I would get it soon and read it. He also said that three cowboys with Parker County connections were used for the book. I continued with my historical markers.

As the movie, *"Lonesome Dove"*, was being aired, the same man arrived at my office and asked if he brought a bus load of people from the Palo Duro Canyon area to Weatherford would I conduct a tour of the

Old City Greenwood Cemetery where Loving and Ikard are buried. I agreed to do so.

He then told me that the Lonesome Dove Movie would be on T.V. that night. Of course I watched. The gentleman never returned with a bus and visitors and I never heard from him – direct – again.

The next day after this second visit I received a call from the Star Telegram asking for permission to come to Weatherford and interview me, about the connection of the three Parker County Cowboys with "*Lonesome Dove*". The next day my phone began to ring from newspapers "all over". It seems it went out on the AP that I knew something. The only thing I could do was share what my "visitor" had told me. It seemed to be what people wanted to hear. I tried to contact Larry McMurtry but was unsuccessful,

Now, I feel I was used for advertising for the "*Lonesome Dove*" fictional book and movie. And, I feel this book about the true legends of the three famous cowboys in Larry McMurtry's book and movie will find its place in not only Parker County but, anywhere readers want to compare truth with fiction.

When Leon Tanner and I started our publications of Parker County History in 2002 under the auspices of NEBO VALLEY PRESS, I told him about my experience and about my research on Bose Ikard. He went with me to meet Ikard and Ann Smith in Wichita Falls and thus began his plans for the publishing of this book in conjunction with Ikard Smith's story "*The Real Lonesome Dove*". (Section I)

"Keep Smiling, Please!"

Nebo Valley Press

Parker County Legends
Trail Bosses and Wild Hosses

Table of Contents

Section I

"The Real Lonesome Dove"

By Ikard Smith

The Real Lonesome Dove

Or

Truth Can Be Stranger Than Fiction

by Ikard Smith

In 1985, I was given a birthday present that turned out to be quite memorable. Not only did it add greatly to my knowledge of my Clay County forebearers and other ranching pioneers, and not only did it send me across the state and back to verify information that resulted in a new state historical marker – which I had the pleasure and honor to personally dedicate- I have to admit that this birthday present did something more. It opened up a chapter in my life that has been pure enjoyment for me leading me to research a somewhat untold part of the history of this area.

In case you were wondering, that birthday present was a book.

I was given *Lonesome Dove*, which at that time was Larry McMurtry's latest offering. Now everyone knows who Larry McMurtry is, but I admit I had only read two of his books before this one. I did notice something, however, about both of those books. He seemed to enjoy blurring the line between fact and fiction. There were great stories in his books, but were they the truth of just the imagination of a gifted novelist? Or a little of both?

In the case of *Lonesome Dove,* I simply read it and enjoyed the marvelous story. McMurtry never claimed it was a true story. In fact, it received the Pulitzer Prize for fiction that year, and, of course, was made an Emmy award winning mini-series on TV.

The characters you know, Gus McCray and Woodrow Call, ex Texas Rangers who take off on an adventure-plagued cattle drive in the late nineteenth century, and along for the ride is their trusted companion, a former slave named Josh Deets.

What you may not know is these characters were based, in part on three real Texans, Oliver Loving, Charles Goodnight and a black cowboy named Bose.

And as you'll soon discover, the REAL story of *Lonesome Dove* is almost as exciting as the book and in some ways it's even more dramatic. For reasons that will soon be clear, I'll concentrate on the story of Bose, regarded now as possibly the greatest cowboy, black or white, that ever saddled a horse.

In doing my research on the real story of *Lonesome Dove,* I also discovered a somewhat startling fact. That is, that I had a personal connection to one of the characters in this real life drama, and it wasn't one of the characters I would have initially suspected.

While it's a sad fact, the truth is every former slave had a former slave owner. In Bose's case his former owner was my great grandfather, Dr. Milton Ikard.

Here then is the story of Bose Ikard, who took my mother's family name upon being freed, and the story of my amateur sleuthing that led to the creation in 1990 of a Texas Historical Marker erected in Bose Ikard's memory.

For me, this story begins when I was rather young. I remember very clearly going to Henrietta to visit my grandparents, Mr. And Mrs. W. S. Ikard. Of particular interest to me were six oil paintings, portraits, that hung is their living room, which they referred to as the 'parlor'. In any event, these full length paintings were of my grandmother and grandfather, and on either side of them, were painted busts of each of their parents. My grandfather, W. S. Ikard, died in 1933. I should tell you that S in the name stood for Susan, but that's another story entirely. My grandmother died in 1937.

These being my mother's parents, she inherited certain things including one of the six paintings. This portrait hung in her house until her death in 1963, and, somewhat through the luck of the draw, I inherited the painting. As you might have guessed, the painting I have been staring at since I was a child, that was in the house I grew up in, and is now in my living room, was none other that Bose Ikard's former owner, Dr. Milton Ikard, my great grandfather.

You might say one of the clues to unearthing the *REAL* story of *Lonesome Dove* had been right under my nose for quite some time.

Now, I want to make sure, at this point in the story, that you've got these characters straight, because I know genealogy can be confusing. Dr. Milton Ikard was by great grandfather.

Picture a somewhat skinny Col. Sanders and you can picture the painting I've been staring at for years and years. His son, W. S. Ikard, the original 'boy named Sue' was, as I mentioned, my grandfather.

W. S. was born in 1847, in Mississippi. His father, Dr. Milton Ikard, saw opportunity waiting in Texas and in 1855 moved everyone and everything to North Central Texas. This included five sons and four slaves including young Bose.

Even before the civil war, Bose was highly regarded by our family as I distinctly remember being told stories about him when I was a child. Of how he, in the words of my mother, grew up with the family, was a playmate to W.S. Ikard, and that he chose to work for W. S. Ikard after he was freed.

But what stood out for my mother, and remember she was telling me these stories forty, fifty, sixty years ago, was how successful Bose had become, not by the amount of money he had made in life, but by the outstanding reputation he had achieved as a cowboy.

To explain how this happened, we need to pick up the story of my grandfather, W. S. Ikard. At this point in his life, he was a very successful cattleman in this area of North Texas. His ranch, the V. Bar, consisted of over 200,000 acres, most of it along and near the Red River. He was an innovative rancher, and in 1876 he traveled to Philadelphia to look at a foreign breed of cattle he was considering buying.

He liked what he saw and shipped them to Ft. Worth on the railroad. However, he was concerned about their ability to last the rigors of a cattle drive from Ft. Worth to Henrietta, so he had them loaded into the back of covered wagons and drove them to Henrietta that way. His concerns were well founded, none of the herd lasted the winter.

The next year, he did the same thing, and that year, the cattle survived and ultimately thrived. What breed had he bet on? Herefords, from the Royal Herd of England. These, in fact, were the first Herefords brought to Texas. Like many ranchers though, in spite of his successes, he had severe financial reversals and his ranch was finally sold to pay debts to a Kansas City bank.

But I'm getting slightly ahead of myself. Back when he was starting out, around 1865, my grandfather wrote a letter on behalf of Bose to one of his friends, the now legendary Texas cattleman, Charles Goodnight, who was living in Weatherford.

Today, we might call this a letter of recommendation, for Bose was apparently ready to change jobs. Do something different. Perhaps he was even looking for adventure, for that's what he surely got.

Goodnight, along with Oliver Loving, would blaze the famous Goodnight Loving Trail from Weatherford through New Mexico and up into Colorado and Montana. They did it with Bose Ikard right by their side, every step of the way.

Looking back on it, this was basically all I knew about Bose. He had been a slave owned by my great grandfather. He had grown up with my grandfather and was considered almost a family member. And then he had gone off on the great cattle drives working as a cowboy for Charles Goodnight, who I didn't know that much about, either. I also didn't know my grandfather knew Goodnight.

So you can see how little I knew about all this, but truth be told, none of these thoughts were in my mind as I read *Lonesome Dove.* When I finished it, I thought it was a pretty good book, but that was it. I no more made the connection between Woodrow Call and Charles Goodnight and Gus McCray and Oliver Loving and Josh Deets and Bose Ikard, than well, the man in the moon. I hadn't even thought of Bose Ikard in years.

That all changed four years later and rather suddenly. I attend the Floral Heights United Methodist Church and during a Sunday

School Class discussion in the fall of 1989, the biblical name Boaz came up. That sparked my memory of Bose. I was sure he was named after the character in the bible, so I gave a brief, and I mean very brief talk during the class telling what I knew about him. I was sure no one had ever heard of him before. And that was the end of it.

Well, the very next week, the first shoe dropped. A good friend of mine, David Lingle, told me he had read a short summary of Charles Goodnight's life in a book by the famous Texas author J. Frank Dobie. In it, he told me, Goodnight had mentioned Bose, by name, several times. Hmm, I thought. In a short biography of Charles Goodnight, the author, J. Frank Dobie, thought it was important enough to include several comments about Bose. That seemed pretty significant, and it started to rekindle my interest in Bose.

Then the other shoe dropped. That same week another friend called from Fort Worth with a strange question. He wanted to know if I knew anything about a man named Bose Ikard.

Well, I was a little shook up, as you can imagine. It seems that an article had appeared in the Fort Worth Star Telegram stating that people were starting to go to Weatherford, Texas to visit the grave site of Bose Ikard. My first reaction was, "Bose Ikard is buried in Weatherford? And people want to visit his grave site?" This was certainly news to me.

The newspaper article went on to say, my friend told me, that the head of the historical society for Parker County, Mary Kemp, had made the connection between the story of Lonesome Dove and the real life adventures of Goodnight and Loving. Since it was fairly well known among history buffs that Loving was buried in Weatherford, and since *Lonesome Dove* the mini-series was being filmed at that time, people wanted to see where Loving was buried.

As it happens, Oliver Loving and Bose Ikard were buried in the same cemetery in Weatherford. And as you'll find out, <u>when</u> these two men died becomes critical to understanding their connection to the *Lonesome Dove* story.

Still at that time, I really didn't know if Bose Ikard's life had been the basis for the character Josh Deets, and I didn't know much about the story of Goodnight and Loving. The only way to find out was to go to Weatherford.

AND I DID.

But first I made a phone call to Mary Kemp, the local Parker County historian who had been quoted in the paper.

I introduced myself over the phone. And her first question, right out of the bag was, "Stop, are you a black Ikard or a white Ikard?

Well, I was a little shook up, as you can imagine. I was to find out later, however, that Bose Ikard had married and had grandchildren and great-grandchildren in the area, so from her perspective, it was a natural question.

After we had established what kind of Ikard I was, I quickly realized she had a lot of information about Bose after he joined Goodnight and Loving's cattle company, though I knew things she didn't know, about Bose's history.

Within a few days, my wife, Ann, and I met with Mary Kemp and her husband, V. Kemp, Jr., and Cleo McQueen, a great grand-daughter of Bose Ikard in Weatherford.

The first thing we did was to drive a few more miles down the road to a small country cemetery, Cox Cemetery near Millsap. Neither of us had ever been there before. There we saw the grave of someone you've probably forgotten about by now. The man who started it all, had brought Bose as a young child from Mississippi to Texas – Dr. Milton Ikard. It seemed fitting they should rest within a few miles of each other.

Over the course of that afternoon I found out much about Goodnight, Loving and Bose Ikard and Mary Kemp's theory that McMurtry had based Woodrow Call on Charles Goodnight, Gus McCray on Oliver Loving and Josh Deets on Bose Ikard. I believed her now, but I wanted to know more.

The first book they encouraged me to get was *Charles Goodnight, Cowman and Plainsman* by J. Everts Haley. I found the book in a local bookstore in Wichita Falls. It had been initially published in 1936, but this was the 11th edition. The point is, this book is still available, and I highly recommend it.

As I was reading this book, I begin looking through another book, one we have had in our family for many years, entitled *The Cattle Industry in Texas* published in 1895. This book, published almost 100 years ago, details a story about Loving and Goodnight that happened in 1867. It seems a year earlier, in 1866, Goodnight and Loving had made their first trail drive up the Goodnight Loving trail from Weatherford to Colorado and back. It was a very successful trip.

The next year, they attempted the trip again, and disaster struck. I should mention at this point, that while this book did not mention Bose, it turns out that he was on both trips, in fact he rode with Charles Goodnight from Texas to Colorado on four separate cattle drives. The important role he played will be described in a moment when I'll quote from Charles Goodnight himself.

But back to our story of the ill-fated cattle drive of 1867. When they pushed the herd within 250 miles of Fort Sumner, New Mexico, Oliver Loving and a cowboy named "One-Armed" Bill Wilson (we can imagine how he rolled a cigarette) decided to ride ahead. Loving thought he could get a better contract on the cattle if they could deliver them early, plus he had unfinished business from the previous year.

Three days out, however, and still miles from Fort Sumner they were attacked by Indians. Taking a defensive position at the bend in Pecos River, these two men held off over 80 Indians for two days. Loving was wounded. At this point, "One-Armed" Bill Wilson decided to go for help, to try and make it back to Charles Goodnight and so he escaped, floating down the river at night.

Loving waited out another day, became desperate, and tried his escape, heading up river. For five days, he was without food, and his wound was getting worse. Finally, he was found by some Mexicans, who for $150, which was quite a sum in those days, took him to Fort Sumner.

Shortly thereafter, Goodnight and the rest of the cowboys were able to bring the herd to Fort Sumner, but Loving, his partner, was in bad shape and growing worse daily. Infection set-in from the Indian wound.

Loving was to die shortly, and was buried in New Mexico, but he made Charles Goodnight promise him three things on his deathbed. The first was rather unusual. Loving insisted, that on the return trip, after Goodnight had gone to Colorado and come back, he was to exhume his body and take it back to Texas. There, Loving requested, that he be given a Masonic burial. Finally he asked Goodnight to consider him a partner, even after his death, until all of Loving's debts were repaid so his obligations wouldn't be a burden to his wife and family.
Charles Goodnight agreed to all three requests, and carried all three of them out.

On the return trip, they took possession of Loving's casket, put it inside a metal container, put it in the back of a wagon, covered it with charcoal, and had a six mule team bring it back to Weatherford, /Texas where his body is buried today.

This incredible story is told in detail in both books I mentioned, Haley's, *Charles Goodnight, Cowman and Plainsman,* and in the 1895 edition of *The Cattle Industry of Texas.* And of course, a version of this story is told in Larry McMurtry's *Lonesome Dove.*

I was now convinced. *Lonesome Dove* was based on a historical event. But how exactly was Bose Ikard involved? And how was he regarded? The character in the book, Deets, dies on the disastrous cattle drive, but I knew from seeing the real grave, that Bose had lived well into his eighties, and had not died until 1929. What again was the real story of Bose Ikard?

As I finished reading the book on Goodnight, I decided I must talk to the author, Mr. Haley, because in his book, Bose is mentioned several times. So I contacted J. Everts Haley, who was then 91, on the phone and told him who I was. No, he didn't ask what color Ikard I was.

He would gladly let me have a copy of the interview, but only if I came to Midland and visited his Library. No material could leave the library, but you could make copies. As you may have suspected, he turned out to be a fascinating man to visit with, a living historian who was old enough to remember many of the things he had written about.

From his written notes made from his interview with my grandfather, I discovered that his father, Dr. Milton Ikard, had first settled in the Weatherford area for a time. This surprised me, as I had just assumed that the ranching operations had always been around Henrietta. This, however, explained certain things. For example, Dr. Milton Ikard apparently knew Oliver Loving, who lived in Weatherford, and sold him one of his slaves taking his payment in cows and calves. This was the start of the family's cattle business.

There were other connections. W. S. Ikard, who was then a small boy, attended school taught by a Miss Molly Dyer. He apparently had great respect for her, and remembered her fondly later as an adult. She married Charles Goodnight.

So you see these three families, the Goodnights, the Lovings and the Ikards knew each other as early as 1855. My visit with Mr. Haley revealed many other things.

He told me that Goodnight had made four cattle drives, the first in 1866, the now famous one in 1867 and then again in 1868 and 1869. Bose Ikard rode on all four cattle drives with Charles Goodnight, and the two developed an extremely strong bond forged in adventure and admiration.

The words of Goodnight himself say it best. QUOTE: He was a good bronc rider and an exceptional knifer, good with the skillets and pans, and according to his boss surpassed any man in endurance and stamina. There was a dignity, a cleanliness, and a reliability about him that was wonderful. He paid no attention to women, his behavior was very good in a fight, and was probably the most devoted man to me that I had. I have trusted him further than any living man. He was my detective, banker and everything else in Colorado, New Mexico and the other wild country I was in. The nearest and only bank was in Denver, and when we carried money, I gave it to Bose. We went through a terrible drought those four years on trail and while I had a good constitution and endurance, after being in the saddle for several days and nights at a time on various occasions, and finding that I could not stand it no longer, I would ask Bose if he would take my place and he never failed to answer me in the most cheerful, willing manner and was the most skilled and trustworthy man I had. UNQUOTEs.

They remained close friends for years. As it turned out, Goodnight outlived them all even Bose. For his marker in the Weatherford Cemetery, not 30 yards from the final resting place of Oliver Loving, Charles Goodnight had these words carved:

"Served with me four years on the Goodnight Loving Trail. Never shirked a duty or disobeyed an order. Rode with me in many stampedes. Participated in three engagements with the Comanches. Splendid behavior."

Signed: Charles Goodnight

For what it's worth, with the exception of the prase "Goodnight Loving Trail", these are the exact words that Larry McMurtry has his character Woodrow Call carve on the marker of Josh Deet's tombstone in *Lonesome Dove*. So you see, the circle is complete.

Larry McMurtry used as his source material one of the great-unsung episodes of the west. The bigger than life characters he created, who for a change were not gunfighters or outlaws, but cattlemen and cowboys were, in truth, and in real life – just as extraordinary as he imagined them. But their day in the sun was over quickly.

Goodnight himself recognized how transitory this whole episode in history was. The era of the cattle drive was over in the blink of an eye, its demise brought about many things, principally the railroad. But Goodnight did not regret its passing so much as he regretted something else he would never have again – his camaraderie with his cowboys.

QUOTE: I wish I could find the words to express the trueness, the bravery, the hardihood, the sense of honor, the loyalty and the trust to each other of the old trailheads. They kept their places around the cow herd under all circumstances, and if they had to fight they were always ready. Timid men were not among them. The life did not get them. I wish I could convey in language the feeling of companionship we had for one another. Despite all that has been said of him, the old time cowboy is the most misunderstood on earth. May the flowers prosper on his grave and ever bloom, for I can only salute him in silence? UNQUOTE.

I would like to close by quoting from the Fort Worth Star Telegram of September 5, 1993 in an article written by Art Chapman. He writes, "Goodnight, Loving and Ikard were gone, relegated to history books were their vast accomplishments where they were crowded out by the tales of the Alamo, San Jacinto, oil gushers, wheeler dealers and politicians. McMurtry helped pull the cowman from their cramped quarters and once again place them on the vast prairie expanses.

Gus and Deets may not live on in McMurtry's continuing works, but they are now firmly part of the Texas myth – too much fiction to be totally embraced. Too much fact to be dismissed.

AND THAT'S THE REAL STORY
Of
LONESOME DOVE
By Ikard Smith

Section II

Oliver Loving
Judy James & Pam Tarpley

Oliver Loving
1812 – 1867

Oliver Loving between 1859 and 1861

A tall, red haired man with piercing blue eyes and a sense of humor was easily remembered. Oliver Loving was such a man. In sparsely populated Hopkins County, Kentucky, on December 4, 1812, Oliver Loving was born to Joseph, a farmer, and Susannah Mary Bourland Loving and was the second of nine children. The county seat of Madisonville had been a town for just two years. In 1833, at the age of 21, he married Susan Doggett Morgan of Muhlenberg County, Kentucky. A small person, three years his senior, Susan had been raised on a plantation in an affluent family setting.

Her parents, John and Jane Irvin Morgan, were of Welsh descent. John had been elected the first representative in the Kentucky Legislature from Muhlenberg County. As a girl, Susan did not to learn to cook or sew; in fact, she never learned these tasks even during her life on the frontier. Oliver and his older brother James married sisters, Susan and Margaret. The two families continued to be very close as they farmed in Muhlenberg County, Kentucky, for the next ten years.

Move to Texas

While Texas was a Republic, an uncle of the Loving brothers settled near the Red River close to the Indian Territory. In 1845, after a visit with his uncle in Texas, Oliver returned to Kentucky and told Susan of the land in Texas. At this time, the nation was gripped with the news of the possibility of Texas becoming a state. So Oliver, his wife and five children, along with his brothers and extended household, decided to make the move to the new state of Texas and the wide open frontier. They set out to join the Peters Colony Settlement which had begun on August 10, 1841, when an agreement between the Texas Land and Emigration Company and the Republic of Texas was made to start a settlement in East Texas. This colony began in the fall of 1842, when Phineas J. Johnson and Henry J. Peters took settlers to the area to begin the colony.

The journey of the Oliver Lovings took the family overland in wagons and down river on flatboats to New Orleans, Louisiana. Family stories remain of the baby, Jane, paddling her feet in the shallow Red River. From New Orleans they boarded a steamboat, which took them back up river to Shreveport. Here they bought oxen and wagons and traveled overland to Lamar County, Texas. With them, they took their household belongings including a Seth Thomas mantle clock, a wooden spindle bedstead, spinning wheel, loom, chest of drawers, cap and ball pistol, featherbed, silverware, cannonball rifle, mortar and pestle, as well as other items.

Their journey west did not stop in Lamar County. After about a year there, they moved to Dallas County.

The 1850 census lists Oliver as a farmer with $1,740 in holdings. James, his brother, was content here in this lush grass and black land and made his permanent home in Dallas County, but Oliver moved to Collin County. He was a freighter, and farmed to feed his family. He hauled freight in his ox carts east to Jefferson to the mouth of the river while other trips took him to Houston.

Soon it became too crowded for Oliver in Collin County. As a freighter, he also made many trips west of Fort Worth to Fort Belknap, near the town of Graham, Texas, and had become familiar with the area.

Because of these trips, he realized the potential of this wide open ranch land. Returning home after one of those trips, Oliver told Susan that there was vast ranching land in Palo Pinto County.

To Palo Pinto County

Onward in 1855, Oliver Loving, his wife, and now nine children, (as Susan had had a child every other year), along with their extended household traveled west to what is now Palo Pinto County. They settled in a remote area northeast of the town of Palo Pinto about two miles north of Salesville in Pleasant Valley which later became known as Loving Valley.

Loving Valley Home

Spurs from the Loving Ranch

Here are the children of Oliver and Susan Loving.

Sarah Irving Loving, born 1834

James Carroll Loving, born 1836

William Willis Loving, born 1838

Susan Mary Loving, born 1840

Jane Eveline Loving, born 1843

Joseph Boling Loving, born 1846

Annie Maria Loving, born 1848

George Barnet Loving, born 1850

Margaret Louise Loving, born 1852

Of these children, Susan Mary and Joseph inherited Oliver's red hair.

The first assessment roll of Palo Pinto County shows Loving with 1,000 acres of land. On this land, the Oliver Loving family built a log cabin home, opened a store on the road to Belknap, and had a Post Office, in which, according to the Postmasters and Post offices of Texas, 1846 – 1930, his son, James C. was the Postmaster. It was Susan's full time responsibility to teach the children to read and write, gain knowledge of literature, and learn the responsibilities of a home. Oliver taught them all they knew about ranching and farming, and through this they learned of his adventuresome spirit. His sons followed their father's footsteps and helped with the cattle while his daughters married men who were also leaders in their communities.

Door knobs from Oliver Loving's Home

Candle molds from the Loving House

Oliver, the Cattle and Horse Trader

Oliver saw the large number of cattle which had come from Spain through Mexico. The Spanish cattle were largely longhorns and by law were free to anyone who would round them up. He knew the potential for developing a market for the cattle. On August 2, 1857, the "Dean of the Texas Trail Drivers", as he was later called, organized the first herd of cattle to be sent out of Texas. For this mission, he entrusted his nineteen-year-old son, William, and neighbor, John Durkee.

William, Durkee, and the men drove the combined herd up the Shawnee Trail to the market in Illinois. At the end of the trail, Will wrote his father that this drive had profited the men thirty-six dollars a head, which totaled a $5,000 profit for the one hundred thirty-nine head. The next year, Oliver and John Durkee, repeated the mission. Oliver also moved herds to markets in Shreveport and New Orleans. Other stock raisers saw the potential of making money on these trail drives, and thus, began the Age of the Texas Cattle Drive.

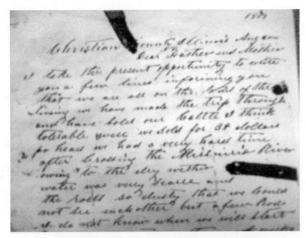

Part of the letter from Will to his parents
written at the end of the drive

In 1858, Loving, John Durkee, Clinton B. Rider, and Preston Witt introduced the raising of horses to the area. They bought them in Mexico for ten dollars a head and drove them to area ranches. This began Parker County's reign as the horse center of Texas. In August of 1859, Loving moved cattle to markets in Colorado and was one of the largest stock raisers in the area.

Drive to Colorado

In 1860, Oliver repeated the trek, and along with his partner and guide, John Dawson, took one thousand head of cattle to Denver, Colorado. They crossed the Red River at the Enoch Steen's Crossing, and then crossed the Cimarron River to the Arkansas River, and onto the Santa Fe Trail. They wintered in Pueblo, arriving two months after leaving Palo Pinto County. In the spring they continued on to Denver to sell beef to the miners in the Colorado Gold fields.

In the meantime, the Civil War had begun. One Texan, whose identity was not preserved, caused a problem in the town by putting a

Texas or a Confederate flag over a Denver hotel. A mob tore it down, and several Texans were thrown in jail, including Loving. The Denver officials would not release him because after finding out about his cattle sale, the Union authorities did not want the gold dust paid Oliver for the cattle to return to benefit the southern states. They detained Oliver Loving in jail for about a year. Only after his friends, Kit Carson, Lucien Maxwell, and others spoke on his behalf, was Oliver released to make the trip home, alone. So that thieves would not think him wealthy, Loving disguised himself and dressed in old clothes. Instead of having the customary matched horses, he had mismatched horses, one large and one small, pulling his wagon. Hidden under his seat in a box was the gold dust.

Return to Texas

When Oliver returned to the Loving Valley, on August, 9, 1861, he found the area deserted. All of the fences were down, the stock missing, and his family and others were gone due to repeated Indian raids. He later found out that the armies had moved out of the area because of the war and lawlessness had set in, both with Indians and white outlaws as well. To protect the Loving family, Henry Belding, a neighbor, had packed Susan Loving and many of her children in a wagon and took them to Weatherford.

Loving went to the courthouse in Palo Pinto to inquire about the whereabouts of his family and found Jesse Hittson, the county treasurer. Hittson was the father of John Hittson, who was the Palo Pinto sheriff and a rancher. Jesse told him that people from the county had escaped the frontier and gone to area towns. Loving went to Weatherford and found his family staying at his daughter, Susan Mary's house. (Dr. David Ford had married Susan Mary in 1856.) With the gold dust Loving had brought back, he had five gold rings made, one for each of his girls.

Nancy and Lewis

When the Lovings first moved to the area now called Texas, they brought with them fifteen to twenty slaves. One of them named Nancy, whose mother was dying, was taken to Susan Morgan Loving's room, when Nancy was three and Susan was a child, long before Susan met and married Oliver. From then on Nancy never left Miss Susan. In Collin County, Nancy married a slave, Lewis, who belonged to a neighbor, Mr. Bowman. When the Lovings decided to move to Palo Pinto County, Mr. Bowman wanted to buy their land on Rowlett Creek. But Oliver would only allow him to buy it if he also sold him Lewis, which was done.

After the emancipation, the Lovings bought Lewis and Nancy a farm near Weatherford. Here they could be near the Lovings and Susan Mary for needed guidance, such as the time Lewis was about to be removed from his church for playing the fiddle and needed advice on whether or not he should stop playing the instrument. Another time, at the beginning of winter, Lewis and Nancy were without food and needed $25 and a load of corn. Susan Mary, whom they called "Miss Sue", made sure that got what they needed. At least thirty years later, one of the sons of Lewis and Nancy, named Charlie, after one of Miss Sue's sons, found out that one of the sons of Miss Sue was starting a business and offered to lend him money. The favors were returned and the family supported, continuing the circle which would last through future generations.

Civil War Days

Oliver spent his time during the war providing for his family, buying land in Parker County, as well as becoming involved with the communities of the area. When he returned from Denver, he wrote a letter to Texas Governor Francis Richard Lubbock, expressing his concern over the growing Indian attacks and stock raids, offering to organize an expedition to take care of the problem. He was also becoming more involved with the Masons and was a member of the Phoenix Lodge in Weatherford. He served on the vigilance or supervisory committee for Parker County and later became Chairman. This committee was organized due to some of the traders not taking Confederate money in payment of debts during war. Historians agree that his committee was made up of some of most respected men in the area. He was also on the first police force in Weatherford organized at a town meeting on February 3, 1862. Other prominent citizens appointed include Samuel Woodward, D. Coon, N. R. Wilson, W. F. Carter, Henry Vardy, T.K. Bailey, H. W. Norton, William Moseley, F. M. Bates, T.U Toler, J. H. Prince, R. E. Creel, D. O. Norton, D. Ramson, J. M. Luckey, M. Upton, J. D. Beckwith and Oliver's son-in-law David Ford.

Oliver's business continued he sold cattle to the Confederate forces along the Mississippi. When the war was over, the Confederate government owed him over $100,000 which he got in Confederate money; this soon became worthless.

Oliver Loving's Gun

Loving – Goodnight Trail

In 1866, after all he had done to take care of his family and provide for them, he now was greatly in debt. The cattle ranges had too many cattle, but there were not enough markets accessible to trail drivers. New territories were sought by stock raisers to take their herds to market. A trip to Colorado, as Oliver had taken before the war, was not safe as the trail he had traveled previously was now under the control of the Comanche and Kiowa.

During this time, Charles Goodnight was rounding up a herd of cattle to take to New Mexico. The two men discussed the situation. Because the Butterfield Overland Mail Southern Route had gone from Texas to California from 1857 to 1861, they talked about taking cattle over this Stage Line, into New Mexico and then into Denver. They knew many of the serious problems that would be along the way – lack of water, Indians, lack of grass, etc. Since both men were consummate adventurers they decided to begin.

On June 6, 1866, fifty-three year old Oliver Loving and thirty year old Charles Goodnight left Fort Belknap with eighteen men and three thousand head of cattle including those branded OL for Oliver and Charlie's O trail brand . The trail they followed went past Camp Cooper, over Fort Phantom Hill, through Buffalo Gap, (which is in the hills just outside of present day Abilene), past Fort Chadbourne, just north of present day San Angelo, across the North Concho, across the Middle Concho, and out on the Llano Estacado for eighty miles to Horsehead Crossing on the Pecos.

This stretch of the drive to Horsehead Crossing, which was named for its horse head shape, was without water and was hard on both cattle and men. On the Concho, they let the cattle drink their fill while the men filled their canteens and water barrels and then began the long

30

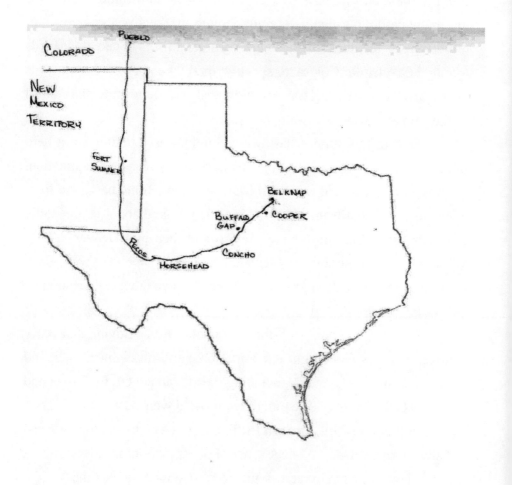

The Loving – Goodnight Trail

three day eighty mile journey. Before reaching the Pecos, lay poisonous alkali ponds that would have meant death for the cattle if they had drunk the water. These had to be averted.

Goodnight scouted ahead and found the ponds. He pulled hairs from his horse and tossed them in the air to check the wind direction. Returning to the herd, he took them in a direction so they would smell the river instead of the pond. The men steered clear of the alkali and pushed on to the Pecos. When finally reaching the safe river, the cattle could smell it for miles. They stampeded; some fell over banks six feet high. Others got caught in quicksand on the treacherous river. When the entire herd had settled down, the cattle was allowed to drink until full on the Pecos. Here the herd and men rested for three days. From here they followed the Pecos to Pope's Crossing, where they crossed the river and went into New Mexico, near what is now Carlsbad, New Mexico. Back on the east side of the river again, they went to Bosque Redondo, named by a grove of cottonwoods by the river, and Fort Sumner.

Marker near the current site

The steers were sold in Fort Sumner for $12,000, but the general stock contractor would not take the rest of the cattle. On July 4th, 1866, celebrating their business deals at Las Carretas Creek, it was decided that Loving should take the seven to eight hundred cattle left into Denver where he could sell them to John Iliff, a well known stockman and long time friend of Loving. Goodnight, in the meantime, would return to Texas to get another herd before winter set in.

Loving took the herd by Las Vegas, New Mexico, up the Raton Pass on the Santa Fe Trail where he ran into the new toll station operated by Dick Wootton on the top of Raton Pass. Wootton wanted a toll for each head and threatened a quarantine to protect the Colorado cattle against tick fever. Loving turned the herd around and traveled back into New Mexico in search of a different route. His men held the cattle for a month while Loving looked for a new route. He found what he considered to be an even better route, which went over a pass near Folsom, New Mexico, and into the area east of Trinidad. They went across the Arkansas River near Pueblo to Denver and sold the herd as planned.

Goodnight and three hands headed back to Texas to buy supplies at Fort Belknap near where his men were gathering cattle on the Brazos River. He packed a mule with provisions and another with $12,000 in gold for the sale of the steers. Each man rode a saddle mule and led a horse behind him. Fearing the possibility of Indian attacks, they rode by night and slept by day. As they entered one of the most dangerous sections of the trip home, a storm came up. In the middle of the storm, the pack animals were spooked and fled. When the storm was over, only the mule with the money was found. The four men had no food for the next five hundred mile trip. When they got to the Pecos, they filled their canteens and got a catfish or two and then pushed on, riding during the day now, as the desert was an unlikely place for Indians. About twenty five miles from the Pecos, they saw something in the distance and believed it to be Indians. Having no place to hide, Goodnight later said he had learned a lesson that day. Here he was with a wealth in gold, yet it was utterly useless with nothing to buy and no place to go to fight the Indians. However, as they got closer, they realized that indeed it was not Indians, but a trader, Rich Coffee, with a load of watermelons. They sat down right there and ate their fill of watermelons. Coffee also gave them some provisions so they could make it home.

After reaching Fort Belknap, Goodnight began gathering cattle for the return trip and was ready in ten or so days with twelve hundred steers. He had learned valuable knowledge on the first drive regarding when to drive and when to let the herd eat and drink. This time they made the trip to just below Fort Sumner in forty days with very little trouble. Loving met the herd there, and they set up a winter camp – the first Texans to ranch in southern New Mexico. They built dugouts and stayed until spring – leaving the area to be used by future cattle drives wintering in the area.

During the winter, the two discussed changing the structure of their business. When they began, the success of the drive depended on their cooperation in driving their cattle to market. Now they completely trusted each other and believed other ventures lay ahead and decided a full partnership could be formed. That winter the Loving-Goodnight partnership began without formal papers but with just a handshake. One hundred beeves (cattle) were delivered to Santa Fe to government contractors once a month and they delivered beeves to Fort Sumner monthly, also. They were beset with problems of contractors going back on their agreements and others trying to outbid them; however, when the winter was over, they had made a nice profit. In the spring of

1867, the rest of the herd was left with James Foster who took the herd west of Capulin Mountain Crater. The two cattlemen returned to Texas for another herd.

Loving went to Palo Pinto County; Goodnight went to the frontier. They later met on the Butterfield Mail line at Cribb's Station and were eager to get started because many other cowmen had heard of the new Western markets opened by Loving and Goodnight. During its use by cattlemen, over a quarter of a million cattle would go to market over this trail.

Third Loving – Goodnight Trail Drive

This new drive had many problems from the beginning. Along with Loving and Goodnight, other drovers included "One-Arm" Bill Wilson, Bose Ikard, Oliver's son Joe Loving, Jim Fowler, H.C. Holloway, "Long Joe" Loving, Yankee Bill, William Taylor, and John H. Kutch. Although they had not seen one Indian on the first drive, they were attacked just after passing Camp Cooper. At this time one of the drovers, Long Joe Loving, no relation to Oliver, was hit in the neck with an arrow. It was removed with pliers after the fight by Fayette Wilson, one of the drovers. The cattle were excited by the Indians and began to stampede. It took a week to round up the cattle. John Hittson and his men were working close by and helped in the round up.

For many miles after that, every night the herd would become excited if they heard a wolf cry, horse, or other sound. In addition, it rained every day between Fort Chadbourne and Horsehead Crossing. After crossing the Pecos, the cattle settled down, but a lot of precious time had been lost.

Loving and Goodnight knew they might miss the deadline for having the cattle in Fort Sumner, about two hundred and fifty miles away. Also, they knew being in Fort Sumner first increased the opportunity for a better price on the herds. Loving wanted to go ahead and be there for the setting of the contract in August, as it was now July. Goodnight was against the idea because of the problems they'd had with the Indians, but finally agreed only if another man would go along with him. "One-Arm" Bill Wilson was chosen, because he was a trusted hand, and Goodnight believed him to be one of the coolest headed men. Additionally, Wilson was married to a step-sister of Goodnight and was a long time friend. Goodnight also insisted that Wilson and Loving travel only at night.

Loving and Wilson Go Ahead of the Herd

For the first two nights, Loving and Wilson followed Goodnight's plan. Loving did not like traveling at night, and since they had not seen any Indians, he convinced Wilson to travel the next day during daylight. On the afternoon of the next day, a band of Indians rode upon the men near the bend of the Pecos River, not far from the New Mexico state line. The two went for the dense brush along the river at the base of a bluff, which made a natural hiding place. They tied their horses and hid under a ledge near the water's edge. The Indians found and took the horses. Just before dusk, the Indians spoke in Spanish that they wanted to talk, so Loving and Wilson cautiously went out. Wilson understood some Spanish and would do the talking while Loving was going to "have his back." But it was a trick. Loving was shot by a bullet that went into his left wrist, breaking bones, and traveled into his side. All retreated to their positions and the siege was on.

Soon, Loving's wounds had caused a high fever, and he believed they would be fatal. Undercover of darkness, Wilson went to the river, about twenty or thirty feet away, and collected water in a boot to try to get Loving's fever down. But Loving urged Wilson to leave, find

Goodnight to tell him two things to relay to his family: first where and when he died and secondly that he would not be captured alive and tortured. He would kill himself by falling into the river. If he survived, he would go south of the river and wait for the arrival of Goodnight. Also, he persuaded him to take a Henry rifle with metal cartridges.
This was one of the first rifles of its kind, and the bullets were waterproof.

Wilson left Loving with all of the rest of the firearms and about one hundred feet away took off all of his clothing except his underwear and hat, buried the clothes in the sand, and floated downstream out of sight of the Indians on guard. It was hard for him to carry the rifle and swim with just one arm, so he buried the gun in the river. When he was safely past the Indians, he crawled out of the water and began searching for the herd and Goodnight – barefoot and through the prickly pear and harsh ground. He found the end of a teepee and used it as a walking stick for his aching feet. Also, when he lay down on the ground, he would awake to wolves around him and he would use the stick to beat them off.

After three days of walking and almost too weak to go on, Wilson found a cave he had located on a previous trip and rested from the sun and his three day, eighty mile ordeal. He continued looking for the herd, which he believed to be headed in that direction. Finally he saw them

W. J. "One-Armed" Bill Wilson

coming. Goodnight and the men saw him, but first thought him to be an Indian because his skin and underwear were red from the dirt. Very cautiously they approached, and realized it was Wilson. They gave him gruel for nourishment, tended to his wounds, and wrapped his badly swollen feet in wet blankets. Goodnight later wondered how Wilson had been able to walk on such badly injured feet.

When Wilson was strong enough to talk, he told how the Indians had attacked, and Loving's wish for him to leave. He relayed where the attack had occurred and how he had buried his clothing and the gun.

Goodnight hurriedly took off with six men. About twenty four hours later, riding through torrential rain, he found the exact location with the buried clothing and the gun, but did not find Loving. He did find a page from Loving's day book, which he always kept in his saddlebags. The page was pinned to a mesquite bush with a mesquite thorn. On it an Indian had drawn a white man wearing a silk hat shaking hands with an Indian. Goodnight later wondered why the Indian put the white man in a silk top hat as no one wore them at that time. They searched the area but found no trails to follow, because the rain had washed away the tracks. He returned to camp believing Loving was dead.

Unknown to Goodnight at the time, Loving had remained on the bank of the Pecos for three days and had crawled his way up the river six miles. He did not go south, as he told Wilson he would, but went up river thinking the herd would be there to water.   He reached the watering hole where he hid under a chinaberry tree and lay for two days. Having not eaten for seven days, he tried to make a fire to cook his buckskin gloves, but failed having nothing to use to start the fire. Finally, three Mexicans and a German boy found Loving. They put him in their ox wagon, and gave him a thick gruel to eat. He agreed to pay them two hundred and fifty dollars to take him to Fort Sumner, about one hundred and fifty miles away.

Ed Burleson, a stock raiser, was riding out looking for his herd and met Loving and his rescuers. Immediately he rode back to Fort Sumner, got the Army ambulance and returned, meeting them about fifty miles from Fort Sumner. The doctor treated his wounds and took Loving back to Fort Sumner.

About two weeks later, Goodnight met Ed Burleson, who had come from Fort Sumner, on the trail. Goodnight told him that Loving had been killed, but Burleson told Goodnight that Loving was alive and healing at Fort Sumner. His wounds were not believed to be fatal. Loving told Burleson that if he saw Goodnight to tell him to go to Fort Sumner immediately.

Goodnight Finds Loving at Fort Sumner

Goodnight hurried to Fort Sumner. When he got there, he found Loving walking around with his arm in a sling. Loving, thinking that he would recover, asked Goodnight to go find some stock that had been scattered below Santa Fe. Goodnight left. When he returned, about ten days later, he found that Loving's wounds appeared to be healing well. However, his arm was becoming infected and gangrene was setting in. Both Loving and Goodnight felt the arm needed to be removed. The surgeon treating him was a young doctor who had been put in charge while the older doctor had been called to Las Vegas, New Mexico. Loving's doctor had not amputated any limbs and was reluctant to do so. Goodnight insisted that the doctor do the amputation, which he finally did. The surgery went well; the arm was cut off above the elbow. Unfortunately, about two days later an artery burst and another surgery was performed to repair the artery. This time the chloroform, used to sedate him during surgery, proved to be too much for his system, and Loving's health began to worsen.

When Loving realized that his condition was critical, he asked Goodnight to make a Mason's promise. Loving asked for two things of his friend. The first was to continue their partnership another two years until his family was free of the debt incurred by the Confederate Army. The second request was for Goodnight to return Loving's body to Weatherford, Texas, because Loving did not want to be buried "in a foreign country" but to be close to his family and friends. Goodnight promised both of these things. Loving died twenty-two days later on September 25, 1867, at Fort Sumner, New Mexico.

Loving Is Buried at Fort Sumner

Loving was buried temporarily at Fort Sumner, and Goodnight went on to Colorado with the herd. Later, Goodnight returned to Fort Sumner along with Bose Ikard, the three Wilson brothers, Loving's twenty-one year old third son, Joe, Bud Willet, and W. D. Reynolds. On their return, Oliver's remains were exhumed. Empty tin oil cans were gathered from around the post, beat out, soldered together and used to line an old-style wooden coffin built of one inch wood. A larger wooden box was lined with charcoal, the smaller box was put inside, and all was sealed. The bed of a wagon was removed, and the casket was set low on the running gear.

The Long Trip Home

On February 8, 1868, the funeral cortege began the slow journey six hundred miles back to Weatherford, arriving at the Loving home on March 4, 1867. On March 8, 1867, Oliver Loving was laid to rest with a Masonic burial in the East Greenwood Cemetery in Weatherford, Texas. On March 25, 1868, the Weatherford Times wrote:

> "Loving's remains have been returned to Weatherford by son Joseph A. Loving. Was buried at Ft. Sumner, New Mexico until February 8. Arrived in Weatherford the 4th and on Sunday 8th burial was by the Masons."

Cumberland Presbyterian Church, 1879

Afterward Goodnight gathered together another herd of three thousand. After the marketing was over, he returned to Weatherford to the Loving home where he kept his promise, and a financial division of the money which the partnership had acquired was made. Goodnight had now fulfilled both of his promises.

Susan Loving

Susan Loving continued to make her home in Weatherford until her death on September 29, 1884. She was a member of the Cumberland Presbyterian Church in Weatherford which later became the Grace First Presbyterian Church.

Her funeral was September 30th, 1884, at the home of Isaac and daughter, Anne Loving Roach in Weatherford. She is buried beside her husband in Weatherford's East Greenwood Cemetery.

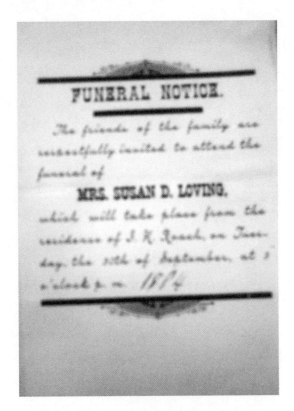

Susan Loving Funeral Announcement

Goodnight's Reflections

Goodnight continued to call Loving "My old partner."

In a letter to Loving's grandson, Goodnight wrote:
"Your grandfather, Mr. Oliver Loving, was more than friend.
He was the nearest to a father to me that I have ever known.
My own father died when I was five years of age and if I
should claim any character or commendable qualities, I feel
I owe it to Oliver Loving. Mr. Loving's character put him
in the class of Great Men, for purity, virtue and high
ideals I have never found his superior. He impressed
all who met him."

Goodnight further described Loving's character –
"Loving was a man that was just as chaste in his language
and manners in the wilderness as he was in the parlor. He
had no bad habits, did not use tobacco in any form and as
far as I know never touched a drink. I don't think he knew
what fear was."

Trail Thoughts

There are many stories about Oliver Loving and his drives, most
of them virtually the same. The most notable drives were to Colorado
in 1861, along with the first, second, and third trip on the Loving –
Goodnight Trail.

In those times, people did not take the time to write things
down; they were too busy living life. Many of the recollections on
which these stories are based were told many years later. Memory has
a way of changing a few of the details. The facts given in this story of
Oliver Loving were written by the authors, to tell the tale by the greatest
consensus of facts. Some stories tell that Loving was shot by an arrow,

not a gun. Stories differ on who were the ones to return his body to Weatherford. The facts do not differ in that his body was brought back over six hundred miles to his home, to be near his family and friends. Facts do not differ as to his greatness, his adventuresome spirit and his courage.

Because of his foresight the stock raisers of Texas found a market for their cattle. He was instrumental in pioneering the Shawnee Trail, Western Trail and the Loving - Goodnight trail, as it was called then. Loving County in West Texas and a town in New Mexico were named for him. A town in near Graham bears his name, two valleys and many river bends bear his. He has been inducted into the National Cowboy Hall of Fame. Oliver Loving was truly a great Texas pioneer from Parker and Palo Pinto counties.

Oliver Loving was a tall, red haired pioneer with piercing blue eyes, a strong sense of humor and will not be forgotten.

Oliver Loving has a star on the Texas Trail of Fame
in the Fort Worth Stockyards

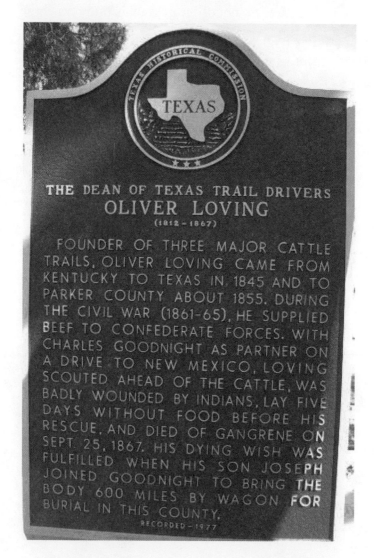

Historical marker at Oliver Loving's Grave

Oliver Loving top, and Susan Loving, bottom photo
City Greenwood Cemetary, Weatherford, Texas

Loving Homestead in Loving Valley

Nancy Haun Dozier, great, great-grand daughter wearing dress of Margared Louise Loving who married Thomas Wilson Margared was the youngest child of Oliver and Susan Loving

These items are from the collection of the
Doss Heritage and Culture Society, Weatherford, Texas

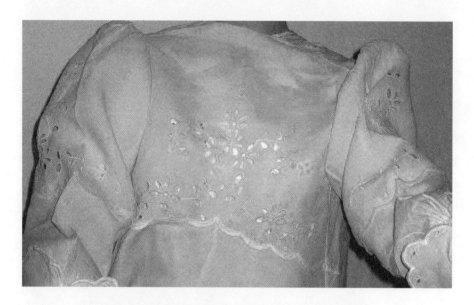

Close up of youngest daughter Margaret Loving Wilson's dress

Susan Loving's Pen and ink well

Fuller Millsap Cemetary in Parker County where two
of the Oliver Lovings' grandchildren are buried

Sources

1. Cullar, Willie and Clytes Anderson, *The Loving Family in Texas 1843 – 1953*, Dallas, Texas: Mrs. James W. Cullar,

2. Dozier, Nancy. Oral Interview, 2007

3. Douglas, C. L. . "Cattle Kings of Texas." The Fort Worth Press April 29, 1935:

4. Gibson, Barbara Belding. *Painted Pole*. 1st ed. Austin, Texas: Eakin, 2001.

5. Grace, John. S. and R. B. Jones. *A New History of Parker County 1906*, Taylor Publishing, 1987

6. Haley, J. Evetts. *Charles Goodnight Cowman and Plainsman*. Norman: University of Oklahoma Press, 1936

7. Hamner, Laura V. No-Gun Man of Texas. 1st ed. Amarillo: Laura V. Hamner, 1935.

8. Holland, G.A. *History of Parker County and The Double Log Cabin*, Weatherford, TX: The Herald Publishing Company, 1937

9. Hunter, J. Marvin, editor. *The Trail Drivers of Texas*. 4th ed. Austin: University of Texas Press, 1992.

10. Jordan-Borden, Edith. History of Parker County Texas Prior to 1936. 1st ed. Weatherford, Texas: Nebo Valley Press, 2006

11. Loving, Oliver. "Oliver Loving to Francis Lubbock." Texas State Library. 1862. http://www.tsl.state.tx.us/exhibits/indian/statehood/loving-lubbock-1862-1.html.

12. Maddux, Vernon R. *John Hittson, Cattle King on the Texas and Colorado Frontier*, University Press of Colorado, 1994

13. Marshall, Doyle. *A Cry Unheard*, Aledo: Annetta Valley Farm Press, 1990

14. *On Our Way Rejoicing. A History of the Presbyterian Church in Weatherford and Parker County 1859-1989*, El Paso, Texas: Gateway Printing Company, , 1989

15. Palo Pinto Historical Commission , Palo Pinto County History. Mineral Wells: 1986.

16. Sammons, Dexter. *Phoenix Lodge the First Twenty-Five Years 1864-1889*. Nortex Press, 1987

About the Authors
Section II & Section III

Judy James is an historian, educator, singer of traditional Western Music, Western radio show host, and a long time Parker County resident. Her love for the West is unending with a real desire that our future generations not forget the men and women who sacrificed to build Texas.

Historian Pam Tarpley comes from a ranching and banking background and has lived in Parker County most of her life. She went to Weatherford schools where she was introduced to the history of Parker County and the West. She, too, feels each generation needs to know our rich heritage and the importance of passing it on.

The authors wish to thank:

✶ Nancy Dozier, a great-great granddaughter of Oliver Loving, for insight into the family.

✶ Kaye Martino and the Doss Heritage and Culture Center for their cooperation and allowing us to take photos of the Loving items

✶ Sherry Brown and Pam Barksdale for their editing of this manuscript

✶ Ann Saunders, Doss Heritage and Culture Center for support, items to photograph

✶ Weatherford, Parker County Public Library staff

✶ Mineral Wells, Palo Pinto County, Boyce Ditto Public Library staff

Keeping Our Western Heritage *ALIVE!*
www.judyjames.com

Section III

Charles Goodnight

Judy James & Pam Tarpley

Charles Goodnight
1836 - 1929

Cattleman, inventor, and Texas icon, Charles Goodnight, was ahead of his time. Born on March 5, 1836, on the family farm in Macoupin County, Illinois, Charles' birth date was three days after the day Texas declared its independence, a fact of which he was proud and to which he would frequently refer. His family consisted of parents Charlotte Collier and Charles Goodnight Sr., Elijah, who was four years older, Elizabeth, two years younger and Cynthia, four years younger.

When Charlie was five, his father died of pneumonia and was buried on the county line between Mancoupin and Madison counties in Illinois. Soon his mother married a neighbor, Hiram Daugherty who had children of his own. After his daily chores were completed, he found time to explore. Explore he did. Living on a farm at the edge of the woods, Charlie spent much of his time learning from nature and observing the wild animals and plants. His mother thought him lazy and said he was spending his time daydreaming instead of working.

Charlie attended school for only a brief time when he was seven, but his teacher gave him a thirst for knowledge which he never lost.

Texas Bound

The rumor of Texas becoming a part of the United States was exciting news, even in Illinois. Many men talked of going to this new fertile land as did Hiram, Charlie's step father. Acting on what he heard, Hiram loaded his family and their belongings on two wagons, joined a wagon train of neighbors, and headed out to their new land in 1845. It was a hard journey, and Charlie rode along side the wagon on his horse, Blaze. He was no exception to many young men of the time; he didn't have a saddle or a blanket so he rode bareback all the way to Texas. Their trail took them across the Mississippi River at St. Louis, and on to Springfield, Missouri. There they ferried across the Arkansas River and then across the Red River. They passed near Paris, Texas, and on to Dallas.

One night the wagon train travelers set up camp on the Trinity River near Dallas. While they were eating, Hiram saw a magnificent buffalo standing in the distance with a lone star shining above. The members of the camp stopped and looked. Before long, everyone went back to what they were doing, but not Charlie. He continued to gaze, captivated by the animal. Concerned her son might get too close, Charlie's mother called him away. This first encounter of the buffalo would not be his last.

Milam County

Many in the wagon train stayed near Dallas, while some others went on west. Hiram, however, turned south looking for the "perfect" spot to set up his home. They crossed the Little Brazos and on to the main Brazos at Old Nashville. Here they cleared a spot, cut trees, and built a log house. The floor was made of planks, and the roof was made of clapboards. There was one window in the large room and one in the loft. Being in Indian country, the cabin was built to withstand an attack. Charlie's room was in the loft; at night he loved to look outside and study the stars in the sky.

Eventually Hiram and Charlotte realized they could no longer live in the same house. Hiram took his children and left, moving into Washington County. Charlotte was left pregnant and alone with her children in the little cabin. Just a few months later, Lucinda was born. To make ends meet, Elijah, the eldest child worked for a neighbor, so it became Charlie's place to do the chores as well as do odd jobs for a nearby merchant. In 1848 they moved from Old Nashville to Port Sullivan which sits on a bluff near the Brazos River. (Neither of these Milam County towns exists today.)

Charlie spent time exploring the woods near his home. One day, during a snow storm, he was looking for an old sow that had disappeared. Soon he found her and her litter. Fearing the piglets would freeze, he brought the litter back home. By the time Charlie returned to the sow, he found the piglets had returned to their mother before he had. This observance of nature helped mold the young Charlie Goodnight.

John Poole, a local stock raiser, gave the young thirteen year old boy a job and served as a stable male role model. In 1853, Adam Sheek, a Methodist minister, moved to the area along with his children. After their marriage, Charlotte's last name was changed to Sheek.

Charlie and Wes Look for Adventure

Charlie and Adam's son, Wes, soon became close friends. Gold fever had hit California by this time and Charlie, who was now nineteen, and Wes talked about heading west and seeking their fortune in gold.

Westward they headed, but upon reaching the San Saba River, they found the river too high to cross. After waiting a few days, they became tired, bored and wondered if they had made the right decision. Not enjoying their first time away from home, the two men decided to head back. Later they talked with Claiborn Varner, who was a brother-in-law of Wes. He had a herd of cattle with over four hundred head he wanted to sell to the boys. Having no money, the boys agreed to take care of his cattle and in exchange they would get every fourth calf.

In 1857, Wes and Charlie took the Varner cattle up the Brazos River into Palo Pinto County to the Keechi Valley, near Black Springs which is now called Oran. At this location, they were a day's ride from Fort Belknap, a day's ride to Camp Cooper (once the post of General Robert E. Lee), and a day's ride to the most important town of the area, Weatherford. This town was the commerce center, the arts center and the cultural town of the area. Wes and Charlie built a cabin in the Keechi Valley and the next year their parents, Adam and Charlotte Sheek, moved to there. Many other people, as well, were moving to settled areas for protection from the Indians.

Marker at Black Springs

Wes stayed with the herd, which was a few years from making them money, while Charlie began freighting. Many of his trips took him to Houston. Soon Wes married and more of the responsibility of the herd fell on Charlie. This was a responsibility gladly taken. Charlie renewed the contract with Claiborn Varner but the CV branded herd soon outgrew the Keechi Valley. New land was found further north.

The Making of a Scout

By this time, a company of Texas Rangers was stationed at Fort Belknap. Charlie's knowledge of the area and his horsemanship were perfect for their need of a scout. He was called on from time to time and enjoyed the company and the adventure. General Baylor, stationed at Fort Belknap, became comfortable with Charlie's skills and called on the young stock raiser often. Many years later, Goodnight wrote in a letter describing the duties of a good scout.

First, he must be born a natural woods-man and have the faculty of never needing a compass except in snow storms or darkness. His eye sight must be perfect, as a plains man he must be able to see as far as any Indian. He must have the faculty of being absolutely cool under all conditions, surprises should not flustrate (sic) him. His coolness and presence of mind to not only protect himself, but those under him. His bearing must be perfect, not only perfect but trained to the precision of the operator on the telegraph. To read sounds correctly, will have much to do with his ability – as much of his experience will be in exploring wild and untrodden countries. He must be able to judge ahead of him as far as he can see, the development of the country, taking the way that has the least resistance to his command, keeping them out of sight as much as possible, in other words picking the routes that will expose him the least to the enemy. He should be able to judge fairly accurate by the course that would take him to water. He should be familiar with every grass or shrub that indicate water or its nearness thereof.

He should be able to watch the animals, if any, and from them learn where the water is. He should be able to judge whether the wild animals are coming or going to water, also he should be familiar with the birds of the territory he is in, and observe whether they are going from or to water, and know those that have water each day. The easiest of all the birds is the one known as the "Dirt-Dobber", if his mouth is empty you may know he is going to it, and he goes straight. If he has mud in his mouth you know he is coming from water.

He must be able to decide instantly what to do in cases of emergencies. He must do the right thing or he may have lost out. He must have the faculty of reading men accurately and must have their full confidence, in other words, they must have faith in the guide. He must have the faculty of not only seeing the tracks or other evidence of the Indians he may find, but he must have the faculty of judging accurately how long it was done, to do this he must be accurate judge of the temperature and effect of the sun. If a blade of grass or herb is cut he must know about how long it has been drying. If water is slack he must know about how long it has been done. It is easy to tell whether a track is made before or after daylight. If a track is made before day light or during the night, it will be full of minute insect tracks or marks, this is so in the desert as well as other places; by getting the eye close to the ground you can easily tell whether they have

been through the tracks, if so, the track is made
before day. You must be able to tell whether the
horse had a rider or riders, which is easily done.
If you are trailing one horse and man you happen
to know the color of the horse and want to test it,
the first time the rider stops, his horse will roll or
wallow – get your eye close to the ground and you
will find the hair, thus telling you that your are or
are not on the right track.

Sound is the most difficult, but the trained
ear should be able to tell the sound, whether it was
made by man or beast or bird. The Indians use
those imitations greatly to locate themselves in the
night, if it is a place favorable for echoes and the
sound give echoes you may know it is made by a
man with out any question, as a human voice echoes
more than all others and is about the only one that
does. Of course on the Staked Plains, we have not
this advantage as there is nothing to create an echo.
But in mountains, and canyons and broken country,
we depend much on the echo. The old Indian
warriors that I have talked to agree with me that no
human can exactly make the sound of beast or bird
I realize that this statement will be doubted, but I'll
ask you how the operator reads the sounds of the
key when they all sound alike to you. The Guide
should also have the faculty, and must have it, to go
from one point to another or to any point where he
has never been. He has the course in his

mind, and he easily goes there. I find this faculty rather uncommon among men, but if he is a proper guide, it matters not how far he is away, and he is instructed to go to a certain point or Fort, he will go straight there. He can go straighter on star light nights than he can in daytime. The sun is troublesome to go by, as it is continually changing its position, and you must get close watch of the time of its course to keep your course accurately. The wind is an uncertain reliance as it may shift any minute. This is only necessary when it's very cloudy – you can test its course by pulling a few hairs off your horse and see which way they drift but after all, the place he has in his mind to go to is his main reliance. He should be able to reach his point in the darkness, and can if he is a true guide.

These are Charlie Goodnight's words and the words by which he lived. It is understandable why General Baylor wanted his services.

Cynthia Ann Parker

One day in 1860, the Indians were raiding the areas around the Keechi Valley. This included Loving Valley (Oliver Loving's home place in Palo Pinto County) and the western edge of Parker County to the Sherman place. Mrs. Sherman was killed and her Bible stolen. Knowing the best material to stuff inside their shield was paper, the Indians took all the paper they could find on their raids. The Indian shield was made of two layers of the toughest rawhide from the neck of a buffalo. After hardening in fire, it became almost impossible to penetrate when filled with paper. On this raid, the Indians had gathered around one hundred-fifty horses.

Goodnight organized a group of men to pursue the raiders. It was raining heavily when the men got together the next morning. They followed the trail and after several days ride, Goodnight found Mrs. Sherman's Bible just before the scout and his party reached the Pease River.

Meanwhile, Sul Ross and his rangers had left Fort Belknap and were also on the trail, heading to the Pease River for a known Indian camp. Goodnight and his men got to the encampment just after Ross and his Rangers. In the fight that followed, according to Goodnight, he saw a squaw, who had been captured, carrying a baby in her arms. As he got close, he saw she had blue eyes. Knowing Indians do not have blue eyes, they believed this woman was Cynthia Ann Parker who had been captured by the Indians in the spring of 1836, right after Texas declared its independence, at Fort Parker near the current town of Groesbeck. They sent word to her uncle, Colonel Isaac Parker to meet them and identify the woman.

Indeed, this was Cynthia Ann Parker. She was taken back to the Piney Woods of East Texas to live with her family. Soon afterwards, her daughter, Prairie Flower, became ill. Cynthia Ann was not familiar with the natural medicines in the East Texas region, and was unable to find what was needed to make her child well. Prairie Flower died.

Cynthia Ann believed her husband Nocona and her son Quanah had been killed. She did not adapt to white woman's life, dying soon afterward, some people say of grief. Later it was discovered neither her husband nor son died in the battle. Nocona died many years later and Quanah became a strong leader of the Indians. Later, Quanah would cross paths with Charlie Goodnight.

Wild Hog Incident

After returning to the Keechi Valley to continue Goodnight's business affairs, news came of the secession of the states and the Confederacy had begun. The South called for men to enlist and Goodnight would have gone, but an incident with a wild hog would not allow it. He, Wes, and their dogs were out hunting wild hogs to get their supply of hog meat for the winter, when one of the largest boars got away from the dogs and ran into Charlie's leg, severely cutting it. When the call for arms came, he was unable to go, but later joined the Frontier Regiment under the command of Captain Jack Cureton to defend the area while the Confederate soldiers were away. The war kept him away from the Keechi valley for long stretches of time. Many months would go by when he did not sleep under a roof, but instead on the hard ground.

Mary Ann Dyer

66

In Black Springs, Charlie's mother's home was the center for anyone who was traveling and needed a place to stay. Charlie wasn't pleased his mother was doing this, but it made her happy. One day, while visiting his mother, Charlie saw a lady he did not know coming toward them. He asked his mother who she was and was told that she was Mary Ann Dyer, the new Black Springs school teacher.

On September 12, 1839 she was born in Madison County Tennessee to Joe Henry and Susan Lynch Dyer. She and her family had moved to Fort Belknap from Tennessee in 1853. Later, Mary Ann's parents died, and it was her responsibility to take care of her younger brothers. After packing up all their things, she moved them to Black Springs so she could teach. It was here she met the young Charles Goodnight, although she had heard about him in Fort Belknap.

When Mary Ann traveled, a few soldiers were with her for protection. Goodnight volunteered for this duty when he could. He also visited his mother more often. In 1864, Mary Ann went to Weatherford to teach, taking her brothers with her. To no one's surprise, Charlie found opportunities to be in Weatherford more often. When in town, he would meet her and walk her to school. Molly was the first woman to

Monument near Carter, Parker County, Texas
two miles north of the Indian Springs Ranch

Ruins of one of the houses Charlie Goodnight frequented,
owned by one of the Sheeks and now on the Indian Springs Ranch
Some say he lived in this house.

catch his eye. He knew she was the one for him, but he had to find a way
to provide for her. Cattle was the answer, he believed. He made plans
to make money for both of them as soon as the area was settled from the
Indian uprisings.

New Trail Drive, Loving – Goodnight Trail

Due to the War Between the States, cattle markets were not
plentiful. The Indians had stolen large portions of both cattle herds and
horses, but wild cattle roamed free. When the war was over, the soldiers
returned to their posts and calm settled over the area. Charlie discussed
taking cattle to market in New Mexico with his long time friend Oliver
Loving. Under a tree in Black Springs in front of Charlie's mother's
house, the two men met to discuss their first trail drive west along the
old Butterfield Stagecoach route.

The tree is still standing in Oran

The two experienced cattlemen knew the drive would not be easy; they would encounter almost ninety miles without any source for good water. Usual trail problems would have to be dealt with like rattlesnakes, weather, and injuries. Other problems for the drive were poisonous alkali ponds and the chance of encountering Indians. The two friends traveled to Weatherford to buy the supplies for the six hundred mile trip.

Historical Commission Marker in Oran

The Chuck Wagon

Charlie knew they would need a way to carry all that was needed for the long cattle drive. From early days, men would carry their food with them for a two or three day journey. If the trip took longer, they would use mules packed with their provisions. Charlie, the inventor, decided they needed a portable kitchen to take on the first drive to Fort Sumner, New Mexico, with Oliver Loving. He hired a cook along with the drovers. The gear of an army supply wagon was taken to a wagon yard in Weatherford and a wagon was built out of bois d'arc wood, (BO' dark) which was the toughest wood known at the time. In many parts of the country this tree is known as the Osage Orange or Hedgewood tree. For the wood the men went to Leonard, Texas, which is northeast of McKinney on highway 69.

The axles of the wagon were of iron instead of wood and a boot of cowhide was hung underneath to carry the fire wood or dried cow chips if wood was not available. On the back he built a box with shelves and drawers in it to carry the cooking supplies. Every item had its place, such as the sourdough jar which the cook used for his biscuits. For the larger items, the large bins were used. The doctoring remedies were in a special drawer. The box was covered with a piece of wood doubling as a work table when in the down position, and as a lid and cover of the box when the wagon was traveling. This lid of the chuck box also had a hinged leg which would be the support for the table. The box was held in place by rods which went through it and were secured to the side of the wagon. Across the top of the wagon, bows of wood were placed, and over the top was a waterproof sheet usually made of canvas. This sheet moved to the cooking area and was known as the kitchen fly when the camp was set up and the cook was at work. On one side was a water barrel which held a few days supply of water. A coffee grinder had its special place too. Cowboys were often asked to grind the coffee. Arbuckle coffee was a popular brand used then and it had a piece of peppermint in it. The cowboy who found the peppermint while grinding the beans got to eat the candy.

Where the first chuck wagon was built is not common knowledge. People of that time were too concerned with their needs and living life instead of writing down locations for future generations. Many believe it was built in Weatherford just south of the square. According to the

History of Parker by the Parker County Historical Commission, Frank Hurst had a blacksmith shop next to the Masonic Building on Main Street. He was a skilled wheelwright, blacksmith, and woodworker. Later on, Clarence Oliver bought the shop and then his son, Guy, continued on the family work. This shop was used to work on chuck wagons.

Chuckwagon

The food cooked for the meals usually was cooked in dutch ovens, which were cast iron pots with legs. These pots were put in the fire; many times coals were placed on top for even cooking. The food included meat which might be fried, roasted or in stew. Beans were staple, canned tomatoes used in cooking would also quench a cowboy's thirst on the trail, and fresh vegetables were included in the meal as they became available. Usually canned fruit was in the wagon for use in cobblers. The cook would fix cobblers as a treat and most meals would include biscuits. Sometimes he would take leftover dough, flatten it, put sugar on it, and the boys would have a cookie.

A special etiquette developed around the chuck wagon. The cook was usually a man older than twenty-two, who knew the ways of the trail. He was in charge of the wagon. Horses were not tied to the chuck wagon, and when the cowboy rode up or rode off, he was to be sure he was downwind so no dirt would fly into the food. Cowboys were not to eat at the chuck wagon table. Nor was there to be any "nibbling or grazing." They would wait for the cook to announce the food was ready. Each would get his food, move out, and let others fill up their plate. When finished with the meal, each cowboy would stack his dishes for the cook. If a cowboy would get up to pour more coffee, someone might holler, "Man at the pot." He then would fill everyone else's coffee cup. The chuck wagon was used through the years whenever cowboys needed to be fed too far from the ranch house for meals. It is still used today. The one first developed by Charlie Goodnight has changed very little from the ones used on ranches and chuck wagon cook-offs today.

On the range and on the trail, the wagon was the center of the cowboy's life. It was his dining room, his bedroom, and the entertainment area as cowboys sat around and told stories. When the cook finished his day's chores, he would move the wagon to face the tongue of the chuck wagon towards the North Star, especially when they were on the staked plains. The next morning, they knew which way was north.

The cook was up first, before daylight, preparing breakfast. When the cowboy got up each morning, he would roll his bedroll and put it in the bed of the chuck wagon. By this time breakfast was close to being served. After the cook cleaned up the breakfast pots, it was time to load the wagon and move on down the trail to prepare lunch, cleanup, and then move on to the supper location, then the process would be repeated.

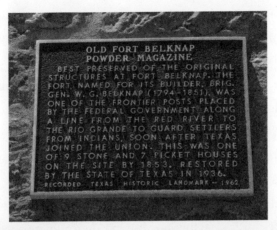

Fort Belknap today

Drives

The complete story of the Loving – Goodnight drives is told in the section on Oliver Loving, but the two men along with their drovers started their first trip to Fort Sumner, New Mexico on June 6, 1866. On the third drive, Oliver Loving was severely wounded and lost his life many days later.

Before dying, Oliver requested Charlie make him a Mason's promise not to let him be buried in a foreign land. (Both men were members of the Phoenix Lodge in Weatherford. The Mason's held a high regard for a man's promise.) Additionally, he asked for Charlie to promise their partnership would continue for two more years and his family be paid half of the

profits. After completing the sale of the cattle at market, Charlie and some of the drovers, including Joe Loving, Oliver's son, Bose Ikard, and others, exhumed Oliver's body. Preparations were made to return it to Weatherford near his family and friends. The second promise was later fulfilled.

Charlie and Mary Ann (Molly) Goodnight

While on the trail, Charlie was not able to be in Weatherford very much to see Mary Ann. After the death of his partner, Loving, the joy of trail driving diminished. He began working in southern Colorado and northern New Mexico building a herd. He established the Rock Canon Ranch on the Arkansas River five miles out of Pueblo, Colorado. While Charlie was in Colorado, Mary Ann went to Tennessee and wrote him a letter from her family home in Hickman, Tennessee asking him what his intentions were regarding their future. Shortly after he returned to Weatherford, Charlie visited with Mrs. Loving and gave her the financial division of the Loving – Goodnight partnership. He then went on to see his mother in Black Springs, telling her he was going to Tennessee to see Mary Ann and marry her. On July 26, 1870, Charlie and Mary Ann, or Molly as she was called, were married at the home of her uncle in Hickman, Kentucky.

Pueblo, Colorado – Rock Canon Ranch

They returned to the Rock Canon Ranch, to make their home. Three of her brothers also worked on the ranch with brother, Leigh, having one-fourth interest in the herd. Molly's first entrance to Pueblo was not very pleasant. Soon after reaching town, they saw two men hanging who had been hung on a telegraph pole. Witnessing this, Molly was astonished and fearful of her future. Trying to soothe her, Charlie said, "I don't think it hurt the telegraph pole." She was very upset and urged him to take her back home to Texas. Charlie asked her to give it a try, and made sure she met some of the finest ladies of the town.

Charlie continued driving cattle. In 1871, he made seventeen thousand dollars working for John Chisum, a New Mexico cattleman. In addition to his cattle interests, Charlie worked hard to make this land prosperous. He built canals for irrigation, brought in fruit trees for an orchard, planted corn, and, basically, turned to farming because he saw a need. Charlie helped build the Stock Grower's Bank of Pueblo, built a meat packing plant in Las Animas, had interest in mining, built Molly a church, and was part owner of the Opera House. Along with other local cattlemen, he formed the first Colorado Stock Raisers Association. He also gave money to start an educational institution. Charlie's cattle business was growing also, and he increased his land holding. Durham bulls were bought in Denver and while they improved his herd, he was able to keep the stamina of the Texas Longhorn. This mix produced a good cross breed for him.

Palo Duro Canyon

Nicholas Martine was a Mexican cattle man who would do

business with Charlie from time to time. Martine told him of a land in Texas where mustangs were numerous. The location was an unexpected chasm in the land on the Llano Estacado or the Staked Plains. Goodnight had to see this land for himself and urged Martine to show him. Off the two men went and Charlie was shown the deep canyon with water, woods, and grass.

This was the place Charlie wanted to make a home for Molly. On his return to Colorado, Goodnight sold part of his interest in the cattle. Unfortunately, the crash of 1873, which began in Philadelphia, had a ripple effect across the country. Charlie lost his money when a run on the bank caused it to crash. Also, a general drought over the Southwestern part of the United States caused a decline in his cattle. They welcomed new opportunities back in Texas.

Charlie sent Molly to visit friends in California while he closed Pueblo the business and moved to the canyon in Texas. Leigh Dyer, Molly's brother, along with Charlie and the other drovers moved the sixteen hundred head left of his herd to their new home in the Palo Duro Canyon.

According to Charlie, the first entrance into the canyon was November, 1876. They went in by the old Comanche Trail, taking them a day to work the sixteen hundred head of cattle down this trail and into the canyon. Next, the men took the wagon apart and lowered it down the side of the seven hundred foot canyon walls by rope – piece by piece. Six months of food was taken down by pack mules to the canyon floor. Arriving at the bottom of the canyon, they were met by a large herd of buffalo. They managed to keep the buffalo away, in order for the cattle to graze.

The first Goodnight home in the Palo Duro was a dugout with cottonwood, cedar logs, and old Comanche lodge poles. Today, it remains within the boundaries of the Palo Duro State Park.

Charlie returned to Pueblo for more supplies and while there met an Englishman, John Adair. The two men discussed Charlie's cattle business. They decided to become partners with Charlie providing the expertise and Adair providing the money.

Dutch Henry

On one of his trips back to Pueblo, Charlie heard of the outlaw, Dutch Henry. Raiding the Palo Duro canyon area was common for Henry, and Charlie decided to make the opportunity to meet him. On his return to the canyon, he sought out Henry and his men, finding them just north of the Canadian River. Riding up alone, unarmed, Charlie told Henry who he was and that peace was what he sought. The outlaw was surprised by Charlie's calmness. The proposal was for Henry to leave the Goodnight land and cattle alone. In return, Charlie would not interfere with Henry's business nor try to follow them. To go against Charlie was to face his well-armed men. Henry was surprised and impressed by Charlie's straightforwardness, therefore; the two men agreed to the deal.

JA Ranch

Back in the Palo Duro, Goodnight checked on his cattle and holdings. A new house had been built, further southeast of the dugout, of native timber without nails. Also built were corrals and a smoke house. Charlie called this the Home Ranch.

Now he was almost ready to bring his wife to this area; however, he realized more supplies were needed. On the way back to Pueblo, he stopped by Sweetwater (which is now Mobeetie in the Panhandle) for his mail, expecting a letter from Molly. After reaching the Post Office, he read Molly's letter saying that she was tired of California without her husband and was ready to go to Texas with him. She would be on the stage to Denver by the time he read his mail. From the letter date, Charlie realized Molly was almost in Denver. Mounting hurriedly, Charlie rode hard, getting there at about the same time she got off the stage.

Plans were made for the Goodnights and the Adairs to go to the Palo Duro. Charlie had an ambulance wagon, which was a special wagon with springs and a mattress on it, readied for Molly to make her more comfortable for the trip. Cornelia Adair, John's wife, rode her own white horse. Also making the trip to the canyon were one hundred head of bulls, along with provisions for six months. When they got to the edge of the Palo Duro Canyon in May, 1877, Charlie had his men put the bulls into the canyon out of the way. Then they began to build roads. The men worked on the road daily going as far as they could each day. On the third day, further into the canyon, they reached a Mesa overlooking one thousand to fifteen hundred buffalo.

Years later, Charlie recalled this first trip to the canyon with his wife. The sound buffaloes make is very loud and in mating season the noise is much greater and was frightening to Molly. Even though the buffalo were many miles away, Molly was greatly concerned and believed they would stampede the wagon and all would be crushed. Charlie tried to convince Molly that the buffalo were miles away, but she was only calm when he built a fire, telling her the buffalo would be turned away by the light much quicker than by soldiers. A few days later, they were able to reach the

bottom of the canyon, and Molly was the first woman to enter the canyon. The nearest white woman, other than Mrs. Adair, was about one hundred miles away and the closest town was two hundred miles away.

The new ranch had begun with the headquarters called the Home Ranch, located on the Prairie Dog Fork or the headwaters of the Red River. Charlie suggested they use Adair's initials and thus the ranch became the JA Ranch. Goodnight's salary would be twenty-five hundred dollars annually payable out of the profit of the ranch. At the end of five years Adair's investment plus ten percent would be repaid and the properties would be divided with two thirds going to Adair and one third to Goodnight.

Old Blue

In 1878, it was time to take the first JA trail herd to market at the nearest railhead in Dodge City, Kansas. The year before, Charlie had bought Old Blue from John Chisum. Old Blue was a lead steer, and was one of a line of special animals. The lead steer would move to the head of the herd and stride out, and the other members of the herd would follow. Charlie tied a bell around the steer's neck and the cattle soon learned to follow the sound. At night, the herd would bed down and the cowboys would put rawhide or grass around the clapper of the bell. Next morning, the rawhide or grass would be removed. When the cattle heard the sound, they would be up and moving. At the end of the drive, Old Blue would lead the herd into the pens and then move out while the herd filed by. Instead of being sold with the herd, he went back down the trail with the cowboys to the home ranch. Old Blue became so tame that he would go to the chuck wagon for treats. At least eight trips were made with Old Blue leading the cattle market, sometimes two a year, and always returning home. Some say he died at the JA Ranch, but others say he lived on into the Goodnight Ranch days and was fed mush by the cooks. His horns hang in the Panhandle Plains Museum in Canyon, Texas. A picture of him is on display at the Armstrong County museum in Claude, Texas.

Quanah Parker

Later that fall, the buffalo had been driven out of the canyon and few remained. Quanah Parker and a band of Indians arrived on the ranch looking for buffalo. A ranch hand saw them and sent word to Charlie. After tracking them down, he told Quanah that he wanted to meet with him in order to make a treaty. A deal was struck, and in exchange for cattle for the Indians, Quanah would keep peace. Charlie later said that he had never known an Indian not keep his word. A longtime friendship began. Later, Quanah Parker, the son of Cynthia Ann Parker, became a peacemaker between the Comanche Indians and the United States. When Quanah wanted to move his mother from her burial site in Texas to Oklahoma, he called on Charlie to help with the United States Government.

Progress on the JA

In 1879, needing a better and more central location for the ranch headquarters, Charlie moved it twenty-five miles east of the old Home Ranch. Here he built a four room house of cedar logs. Also built on site were a bunkhouse, a bookkeeper's house, a wagon boss's house, a blacksmith shop, a wagon yard, and a milk and meat cooler. Later on, Mrs. Adair found a spot to add a two-story, nineteen-room main house.

By 1882, the partnership bought ninety-three thousand acres. Goodnight purchased the Quitaque range in Briscoe County for Cornelia Adair and a post office had been established on the JA. Even with the purchases, the profits amounted to more than five hundred and twelve thousand dollars. The JA Ranch had expanded to include the counties of Armstrong, Donley, Briscoe, Swisher, and Hall. The contract between Adair and Goodnight was extended for another five years.

Each year John and Cornelia Adair would make an annual trip to the ranch. John was always impressed with the progress the ranch was making. Cornelia and Molly enjoyed visiting each other. When John was out with the men, he would order them to saddle his horse or do something else for him. They were not accustomed to this treatment and generally refused. John was indignant that his wish was refused. Charlie explained to him that they were not like the "lackeys" back in England. Here the hired men worked very hard and were treated with respect. One day on a visit, the Adairs and the Goodnights were sitting down to dinner when a cowboy came in; Molly invited him to sit at the table. John Adair refused to eat at the same table has a "hired hand" and told Cornelia that they were leaving. Immediately, they were on their way back to England.

Charlie had a rule that there was no drinking or gambling among his men. Anyone found doing either would be discharged. He believed that both vices would cause disharmony among his men. As a result no one was ever killed because of a dispute while working on his ranch. This rule got close to home when he found that Molly's brother Walter was gambling on one of ranges with the foreman who was Jack Ritchie, son of Cornelia Adair by her first marriage. Jack was removed to second in command and not fired, only because of his mother. Walter and the other men were discharged.

Molly

Molly settled into life on the ranch. The men were busy with the cattle. So during the day she was usually alone. Her brothers all had responsibilities on the ranch so at least they were around her.

She became a very important figure to the men on the ranch. When they were ill or injured, "Aunt Molly" was there for them. She knew the local plants needed to make them well. She knew which plants were needed for each ailment. She loved the area, especially the hoodoos, which were tall rock formations, standing guard over her.

One of the hands gave her three chickens to keep her company. She loved those chickens and said that they would follow her everywhere,

82

come when she called, and talk to her – in their own language.

Riding with Charlie (when he was available) was great
pleasure to both of them. The women of the day rode sidesaddle with
the conventional saddle having a horn for one leg to rest, but not two.
Charlie designed a special saddle for Molly that had two horns. He said
it was more comfortable for Molly and safer for the horse.

When the men were fighting off buffalo to give their cattle
grazing land, and commercial buffalo hunters were in the area, many
times orphan buffalo calves were left. Molly heard their cries and urged
her brothers and Charlie to bring her the orphan buffalo. She kept
them and kept them alive. Soon Molly had her own herd of buffalo
and is credited with saving the buffalo. Charlie, ever the inventor, tried
crossing the buffalo with the cattle forming the "cattalo". The resulting
breed had strengths of the buffalo and cattle. Later the buffalo herd was
moved to the Quitaque range. Not only did she have her own buffalo
herd, she also had her own cattle herd branded with her brand – PAT M
in Colorado, and the Flying T while at the JA. She was partners with
her brother, and, later they sold the herd and the brand.

The men on the ranch respected Molly. She was called the
"Mother of the Panhandle" and "The Darling of the Plains." To show
their appreciation, they gave money to buy her a silver tea service.
Charlie gave her a grandfather clock and had a plaque engraved

> "In honor of Mrs. Mary Dyer Goodnight, Pioneer
> of the Texas Panhandle. For many months, in 1876-
> 1877, she saw few men and no women, her nearest
> neighbor being seventy-five miles distant, and the
> nearest settlement two hundred miles. She met isola-
> tion and hardship with a cheerful smile, and danger
> with undaunted courage. With unfailing optimism,
> she took life' varied gifts, and made her home a

house of joy."

On trips to Pueblo, she found furnishings for the house, including books and pieces of art. She commissioned an artist to draw scenes around the JA and of their home and a photographer to capture the area. Unfortunately the pictures were destroyed by fire.

Washing clothes was a problem on the JA because the floors were dirt and the ever present wind stirred it up. There was also dirt in the water source for washing. Nothing seemed to remove the dingy color from clothes including boiling them in lye soap. Later, deeper wells were dug and the clothes were brighter.

Sundays were Molly's day to hold Sunday school on the ranch. All hands attended, as well as newcomers. The boys made sure that the no one upset "Aunt Molly."

Saint's Roost

One day Charlie left the ranch riding alone to Sweetwater, now called Mobeetie. Suddenly, he rode up on about twenty to thirty people in a tent village . In the largest tent, he heard singing. He dismounted and talked with them. Charlie found out that they had come from New York, seeking a place to call home. This was it. They wanted to open a store and establish a town. Charlie asked who would buy from them because he was their nearest neighbor. They believed that the Lord would provide for them. He tried to dissuade them, but they would not change. He taught them how to build a sod home. They sold lots with the provisions that anyone who bought the town lot would not have a saloon on it. The town was named Clarendon, but many people in the area called it "Saints' Roost."

Bringing the Government Close

During this time, if any official documents needed to be filed, or any official business was needed, Henrietta in Clay County, two hundred miles away, was the closest place to go. Goodnight had a representative there, but the distance was great and communication difficult. An officer of the Texas Rangers was sent to scout out the need for another site of government. In 1880, Mobeetie, on the Sweetwater, became the county seat of Wheeler

County as well as being known as the capital of the Panhandle.

Goodnight and the area men knew that it would take more than a closer seat of government to keep order. In Mobeetie in 1880, the Panhandle Cattle Raiser's Association was formed. Charlie was elected the first president. Each man was given an equal voice, whether he had ten cows or a herd of thousands. The association had a brand inspector who ruled on debates over brands. Equal opportunity was given to all members. Seeing a need for a teacher in Clarendon, Charlie urged the Panhandle Cattle Raiser's Association to hire one, which they approved at their next meeting.

Goodbye to the JA

John Adair died in 1885, and when his widow wanted to continue the contract in 1887, Charlie decided it was time to limit his ranching operation and sell out. Beef prices were falling, the Fort Worth and Denver City Railway had been built, and settlers had come to the area where once it was only Charlie, Molly, and all they had brought to the land.

Charlie had come to the JA to build the best ranch he knew. Starting his herd by crossing Durham cattle with Longhorn cattle, Charlie then introduced Herefords because he wanted to eliminate the horns. Wanting cattle with no horns, he found the right breeds to cross to produce polled cattle, though others scoffed. Noted historian Dr. Walter Bishop of Illinois, who is a long time friend of other Illinois Goodnights, says that the Goodnight cattle were always decades ahead of other cattle.

But now Charlie was ready to have his own place. He wrote

a letter to Mrs. Adair telling her he was going to be leaving at the end of the contract year. The following time was spent running the ranch and planning for and completing the division of interests. Mrs. Adair received more than the contract had called for. Goodnight got the Quitaque Ranch, which he soon sold. In May, 1888, they left the JA. Mrs. Adair continued to take an interest in the JA all of her life. She even insisting that the remuda, a group of saddle horses used in the ranch work, was all bay horses, and that the cattle were Herefords, imported from England.

Goodnight, Texas

Charlie found some land, about one hundred-sixty-seven sections that had not been settled, at the edge of the caprock of the Llano Estacado and by the Fort Worth – Denver railroad line. This was where he would build HIS ranch. He sent a man to Louisiana for the perfect lumber, another to Trinidad for doors and windows, and another to the Dutch Canyon in the Palo Duro for heavy timbers. The house would be a large two story, which is what he had always wanted for Molly. Nothing was spared. Molly would design this house with plenty of rooms and a wrap around porch. The windows would be etched or colored glass. Upstairs he would have a sleeping porch to look out on the stars at night as he did when as a young boy in Milam County, and as he did during his many years on the trail drives. He would also have a den where he could sit and think or whatever he wanted to do. It would be his place in the house.

The home became a place for visitors, some staying a short time and some staying for months. When the housekeeper who had been with them for many years died, a widow lady from Tennessee was hired to work for them. She brought with her an eighteen month old son, Cleo. The Goodnights had not had children of their own and soon young Cleo was following Charlie around wherever he went. He would say, "'Night, what are we going to do tomorrow?" Charlie would answer and he would agree. This boy came to learn more about the cattle and the buffalo than any one else, except "'Night".

When asked what they remembered most about the big house, many visitors replied "the kitchen". This was the center of the house. Everyone was welcome at the table as they always had been. Indians would come from time to time. A story is told that one day at the table with Charlie and Molly were two Indians and Cleo's two year old daughter. The Indians could not speak English, but the baby and the Indians seemed to communicate well,
while the other adults could understand neither language.

The Goodnights loved to entertain. Fruit trees were planted on the land and an orchard grew. Bermuda grass was planted for a picnic spot and July 4th picnics were celebrated. Another time that Molly loved to entertain was at Christmas, and the people came from miles away. The house became almost like a museum and Molly loved to show it off.

With Molly's love for education, she and Charlie started a college at Goodnight. A love for education was in Charlie's family also; his nephew, T. W. Stanley, would later become superintendant of schools in Weatherford. Many of the students at the college were assisted by the Goodnights in paying their tuition. It was not unusual to see a young man coming up the lane leading a cow to pay for his tuition. They also built a Children's home which became a Buckner's Children Home. The town of Goodnight sprang up. People of the town loved and respected Charlie and Molly Goodnight. Both the college and the high school mascots were the Buffaloes. Montie Goodin, the daughter of Cleo Hubbard, said that part of the lyrics to the high school song were "We're wild and woolly and hard to beat. Buffalo meat is all we eat. Go Buffaloes!"

One time Goodnight had a celebration on the ranch and invited Quanah and some Indians to the event. A Buffalo hunt was staged and they had a feast. Quanah wrote, "I am bringing some of the old ones with me; it will do their hearts good to see the buffalo run again." A copy of the letter is on display at the Armstrong County Museum in Claude, Texas.

Molly owned her own cattle here, too. The Dyer brand was the Y Bar brand. Later they gave the brand to Cleo Hubbard and now his daughter, Montie, and her husband Emery Goodin have the brand and live on part of the ranch.

Y Bar brand on the Goodin's gate at the ranch

Charlie's horse was "Old Buttons". His saddle had a flat saddle horn, was two toned, with silver, and had his initials on it. One day, late in life, he got dressed up, Cleo saddled his horse, and pictures were made with him on his horse. He got down off the horse, walked over to Cleo's wife, and handed her the reins. He never rode again. (The saddle is now in the Panhandle Plains Museum in Canyon, Texas.) He used a buggy if he wanted to go anywhere. Stories are told by the family that when Charlie started off somewhere, the children on the ranch would love to go with him because he would let one of them open the gate for him and then toss them a quarter for their work.

Charlie continued to change with the times. When he was in his nineties, he bought a car. He also went into the movie business, making a silent movie at the Goodnight ranch named *Old Texas*.

Scotty Boomer's Reflections

Scotty Boomer was a delightful lady who lived in Claude. When she was ninety years young, the authors had the opportunity to interview her. She said her dad was a good friend of the Goodnights and she loved to go to the ranch. Charlie and her dad would sit on the porch and talk while she would play. Molly, or Mrs. Goodnight as everyone called her, would take her all around the yard and Hollyhocks were prevalent there. Molly would pull the flowers off and give them to Scotty who soon had a washtub full of Hollyhock flowers at home. She remembered Molly Goodnight because of Hollyhocks.

Every July 4th the people of Goodnight were invited to a picnic down on the ranch and it was plum picking time. Molly attended everything as did everyone in the small community of Goodnight which now numbered three to four hundred people. She even went to all of the PTA meetings. On Saturdays, she would go around town in her buggy giving Hershey chocolate bars to all of the children. Scotty said, after Molly's deliveries, it was not unusual to see Molly and her buggy striking out across country to her home, not following the roads.

Her remembrances of Charlie, or Mr. Goodnight as everyone called him, were that he always wore a black suit. His beard had turned from black to white. There was a tobacco stain down it because he always chewed tobacco. Everyone respected him. He was always coming up with something new.

The first dance Scotty went to was on the ranch. All of the furniture was taken out of the house. They danced all night to the music of some of the ranch hands who played guitars and fiddles. At midnight they stopped and ate, but then went back to dancing.

Sadly, Scotty talked of the time in 1926, when Molly died. The funeral was at the Methodist Church in Goodnight and a large crowd gathered there to pay their respects and honor Molly Goodnight. She vividly remembered Charlie Goodnight walking down the aisle to his pew. Just as he got there, he stopped, paused to look at Molly's casket, and a big tear fell from his eye and splashed on the pew.

Trail Thoughts

Three years later, Charlie joined his beloved Molly. They spent a long life together. Half of the Goodnight Ranch in Armstrong County was given to Cleo Hubbard, Charlie's right hand, who had become foreman when was nineteen. Now, that part of the ranch is owned by Cleo's daughter Montie and her husband, Emery Goodin. The house is owned by the Armstrong County Museum with plans to restore the original home.

Goodnight house just off of Highway 287 in Goodnight, Texas

The legacy of Charles and Mary Ann Dyer Goodnight reaches far and wide. Charles Goodnight has been inducted into the National Cowboy Western Heritage Museum as cowman and plainsman. Mary Ann Dyer Goodnight has been inducted into the National Cowgirl Museum and Hall of Fame

They were philanthropists, inventors, and yes, dreamers. From the first buffalo that Charlie saw to the last one, he was a dreamer.

Three Fences

Charlie went back to Illinois and had a wrought iron fence placed around his father's grave. Now there is a large cedar tree growing out of the plot.

Charles Goodnight, Sr.'s grave in Illinois

He went to Black Springs, and had a fence put around
his mother's grave.

Charlotte Sheek's grave site, Oran, Texas
Note the spelling on the grave is Sharlotte Sheek

Today there is a chain link fence around Goodnight's grave in
Goodnight, Texas.
Many cowboys who visit the grave tie their wild rags to the fence.

Goodnight Cemetery, Goodnight, Texas

Charles Goodnight Grave in Goodnight, Texas

Mary Ann is buried beside Charles in Goodnight, Texas.

Leigh Dyer, her brother, is also buried in the Goodnight Cemetery.

Sources

1. Adams, Ramon F. *Come an' Get It, the Story of the Old Cowboy Cook.* Norman: University of Oklahoma, 1952.
2. Anderson, H. Allen. "Charles Goodnight." *The Handbook of Texas.* January 30, 2002. 2007 http://www.tsha.utexas.edu/handbook/online/articles/GG/fgo11.html.
3. Anderson, H. Allen. "Donley County Biographies." February 24, 2000 http://www.rootsweb.com/~txdonley/dbios2.html.
4. Boomer, Scotty. Oral Interview, Goodnight, Texas
5. Brockman, John Martin. "Port Sullivan." *Handbook of Texas.* January, 2007. http://www.tsha.utexas.edu/handbook/online/articles/PP/hrp52_print.html.
6. Crawford, Ann Fears, and Crystal Sasse Ragsdale. *Women in Texas.* 2nd ed. Austin: State House Press, 1992.
7. Douglas, C. L. . "Cattle Kings of Texas." The Fort Worth Press April 29, 1935:
8. Gibson, Barbara Belding. *Painted Pole.* 1st ed. Austin, Texas: Eakin, 2001.
9. Goodin, Montie. Oral Interview, Goodnight, Texas
10. Goodnight, Charles. "First Entrance to Palo Duro." *The Southwest Plainsman* May 12, 1925
11. Grace, John S. and R. B. Jones. *A New History of Parker County 1906.* Dallas: Taylor Publishing, 1987
12. Haley, J. Evetts. *Charles Goodnight Cowman and Plainsman.* 2nd ed. Norman: University of Oklahoma Press, 1949
13. Hamner, Laura V.. No-Gun Man of Texas. 1st ed.. Amarillo: Laura V. Hamner, 1936.
14. Holland, G.A. *History of Parker County and The Double Log Cabin.* The Weatherford, TX: Herald Publishing Company, 1937
15. Hunter, J. Marvin, editor. *The Trail Drivers of Texas.* 4th ed. Austin: University of Texas Press, 1992.
16. Jones, Nancy Baker. "Donley County Biographies." February 24, 2000 http://www.rootsweb.com/~txdonley/dbios2.html.
17. Maddux, Vernon R. *John Hittson, Cattle King on the Texas and Colorado Frontier,* University Press of Colorado, 1994

18. Marshall, Doyle. *A Cry Unheard*, Aledo: Annetta Valley Farm Press, 1990
19. Maynard, Frances Oliver. *History of Parker County, Parker County Historical Commission.* 1st ed., 4th printing, Dallas: Taylor Publishing, 1980.
20. Roach, Joyce Gibson. "Mary Ann Dyer Goodnight." *The Handbook of Texas*. January 30, 2001. http://www.tsha.utexas.edu/handbook/online/articles/GG/fgo35.html.
21. Sammons, Dexter. *Phoenix Lodge the First Twenty-Five Years.* 1st ed. Austin: Nortex Press, 1987.

The authors wish to thank:

✴ Sherry Brown and Pam Barksdale for their editing of this manuscript
✴ Montie Goodin for insight into the Goodnight family and the Armstrong County Museum, Claude, Texas
✴ Dustin Sanders for our introduction and opportunity to interview Scotty Boomer
✴ Dennis Dodson for chuckwagon information
✴ Wayne Ellis, owner of the Indian Springs Ranch, for allowing us to take photos of the ruins, known locally as the Goodnight house
✴ Bo O'Rourke for the painting of Molly Goodnight
✴ Ann Saunders, Doss Heritage and Culture Center for support, and items to photograph
✴ Erlene Finney for pictures

Keeping Our Western Heritage *ALIVE!*
www.judyjames.com

Charles Goodnight
Chuck wagon box

Photo: Panhandle Museum
Canyon, Texas

Charles Goodnight saddle

Photo: Panhandle Museum Canyon, Texas

Section IV

*The Ikards
Black and White*

Leon Tanner & Mary Kemp
Sarah Slee Anderson

Section IV

Table of Contents

Chapter I

Ikard Smith inherited this picture of Dr. Milton Ikard,
and it remains in the Smith Wichita Falls home to this day.

Dr. Milton L. Ikard
(1812-1882)

Dr. Milton L. Ikard and his wife, Isabella Tubb, were born in Franklin County, Tennessee in 1812. They married March 17, 1837 and are now buried in Parker County, Texas near Millsap in the Cox Cemetery adjacent to the Ikard homestead. Isabella died a year before her husband in 1881.

Ikard History by Mrs. Lynn Boyd

Dr. Milton L. Ikard and his wife, Isabella Tubb, moved to Texas from Alabama, Mississippi, and Louisiana in 1852. Dr. Ikard provided for his family by the profession of Hydropathic Doctor, Proprietary Medicine, School Teacher, and Farmer.

When the couple made their journey to Texas in 1852, Dr. Ikard traveled by horseback ahead of his family and settled near Honey Grove in Lamar County. Soon after his wife, Isabella, followed also riding horseback and blazing the trail for the Carry-all which carried their five young sons with their possessions and the former slaves that followed. The Ikards' sons were Lafayette Eugene, Robert Emmett, Elisha Floyd, William Susan, and Milton, (Jr.).

In 1855, they moved to a farm in Parker County about nine miles southwest of Weatherford, Texas. They camped the first winter while building a log cabin with no windows to protect them from marauding Indians. The trees were chopped down with an axe, hewn with a broadaxe, laid in place and daubed with mud. Ventilation in summer was obtained by pushing out the chinks and was winterized by re-chinking.

The schoolhouse and benches were built of logs, the latter split in half. Desks were one long plank running the length of the wall with a bench in front of it. They wrote with faces to the wall, turning about to recite. W. S. said "long hours and hard benches were part of their education, but it was their only opportunity to learn the three Rs which they did diligently."

Until the end of the Civil War, the family was in constant danger. Every full moon the Indians would attack in some section of the surrounding country. The Comanches and Kiowas were most savage in their raids, killing or scalping adults, capturing children and stealing horses. During those days and up to 1875, Dr. Ikard's sons and male relatives were engaged in battles with the Indians either by helping their neighbors when attacked or when they, themselves, encountered the enemy while herding or driving their cattle to market. They saw friends injured or killed but the Ikard family luckily escaped unscathed from these brutal forays.

When the Civil War and most of the Indian dangers were over, a box house with glass windows was built for the family. Green lumber and supplies were hauled from Jefferson, Texas, by ox teams. Lumber cost 50 cents per hundred at the mill.

Dr. Ikard was considered successful in all his endeavors. In 1876 he was elected and served as Representative from the 15th District in the 15th Legislature of Texas. Historical Sketch of Parker County says, "He is an excellent and worthy citizen and much respected."

In 1865, Elisha Floyd and William Susan Ikard went to a meeting of Jack and Palo Pinto County cattlemen at Jacksboro, taking with them the marks and brands of cattle, which had strayed south into Parker County during the winter. They made a deal with these cattle men to feed, herd, and deliver the strayed cattle for $1.00 per head at their father's farm in June, taking their pay either in cash or in cattle. In this way (with two ponies each) they began the Cow Business under the name of E. F. Ikard and Bros., firm of Lafayette, Elisha Floyd, Wm. S. and Milton. They drove one to three herds a year to Abilene, Newton,

Baxter Sprigs, and Wichita, Kansas, until the M. K. & T. built into Denison, Texas, in 1873.

In 1873, E. F. and Wm. S. moved to Clay County (being among the first settlers in the County) and opened a farm about six miles below Wichita Falls on Big Wichita River. They secured range rights near mouth of Beaver Creek on Big Wichita, which they ran until fall of 1881 when severe drought forced them to move to Greer County, Texas, near Doan's Store. Capt. Hall, former Texas Ranger and now Indian Agent at Anadarko, Indian Territory, made a deal with the Ikards that they were to furnish a specified number of beeves annually, work Indians, and pay a specified amount of cash for the use of Greer County.

In 1875, E. F. & Wm. S. bought 20,000 acres at Charlie to put Pure Bred cattle on. They went to Philadelphia Centennial in 1876 and purchased 10 Bulls and 1 Cow of Anxiety Fourth and Garfield strains from T. L. Miller of Beecher, Ill., who was exhibiting them at the Fair. These were shipped to Denison, driven 140 miles to Headquarters Ranch near Henrietta. Three bulls died enroute and five more shortly thereafter with Tick fever. REMNANT WAS FOUNDATION OF HEREFORDS IN TEXAS, their calves being sold at Mobeetie, Pecos River County, Charlie Goodnight of Palo Duro, and in to New Mexico. Ikards paid Quanah Parker $100.00 per month to protect their cattle from Indian raids. "Best money ever spent," said Ikards. (*Dallas Morning News* – Jan. 31, 1940.)

In 1882, Wm. S. Ikard sold his interest in Greer County cattle to Harold bros. And E. F. Ikard who in 1883 sold 75,000 head of good cattle for $22.50 per head, 500 saddle horses, wagons and branding equipment together with lease rights to 1885 on a 50 by 75 mile spread of good grass land in Greer County to the Franklyn Land & Cattle Co. for $1,500,000. With this deal went lease on Railroad lands and a lien on School lands of the 200,000 acres in Wheeler County in the Panhandle.

After selling out of Greer Count interest to E. F. Ikard, Wm. S. bought and fenced 11,000 acres on Red River in Clay County and started a fine stock farm of cattle, putting Texas best cows and Registered Hereford Bulls together.

In 1884 Ikard Bros. bought and fenced 75,000 acres in Clay and Archer Counties and ran about 10,000 head of Texas Longhorn cattle on it, using the original Circle or O Brand first owned by Ikards. $\underline{V}$ (V Bar) was
also used. Headquarters were on V Bar Springs north Mankins.
Foreman of Ranch was L. E. Ikard; Range Boss —Buck Engledow;
Wagon boss — Andrew J. Ikard (son of Seyburn).

Security debts up to $300,000 for Curtis and Atkinson and the severe droughts of 1886 and 1887 caused Ikards to fail in Business. They protected their creditors with mortgages before failure.

After 1889, the Ikard brothers continued in the cattle business individually; E. F. and Miton (Jr.) settling in the Indian Territory: Lafayette, near Nocona, thence to El Paso; Wm. S. continued in Clay County, where he built up his "Sunny Side" herd of Herefords. He was one of the founders of the Southwest Fat Stock Show which is still held annually – was also first president of the Texas Hereford Assn. Six Herefords from Queen Victoria's herd were purchased by W. S. Ikard from Dudgen & Simpson Co. of Illinois who imported them from.

106

England. The horn from one of the animals has a crown on it (the Royal Brand). This horn is in possession of Mrs. Lewis Ikard of Henrietta, Texas.

This Sketch was compiled by Mrs. Lynn Boyd (Edwina Ikard, great-granddaughter of Dr. Milton Ikard) from Genealogical Research Papers of Frank N. Ikard, Washington, D. C.; contracts, letters, cables, ect. Of Francklyn Land and Cattle Co. now in the Historical Museum at Canyon; Texas State Archives; Dallas Morning News; 1860, 1870 and 1880 Census Records; and from W. S. Ikard's writings and J. M. Ikard.

Editors note: Portions of this article were printed in the Weatherford Democrat *Oct. 16, 1966.*

The Cox Cemetery
Millsap, Texas

Ikard Monument

According to the Parker County Genealogical Society's 1998 records, Dr. L. Milton Ikard, his wife, and eight relatives are buried in Cox Cemetery. They are as follows:

Dr. Milton L. Ikard (Feb. 2, 1812-Dec. 31, 1882) and his wife, Isabella Tubb Ikard (Oct. 10, 1812-Oct. 10, 1881).

Malinda Wright Ikard, wife of Lafayette E. Ikard (1845-1889) and daughters Mildred (1885-1939), Isabella E. (1870-1946), Willie May (1879-1966), and Floyd (1881-1966).

Bettie Ikard, wife of Milton Ikard Jr., (March 30, 1850-died Nov. 3, 1880) and their children Robert E. (July 28, 1872-Nov. 16, 1872) and Eula M. (July 26, 1876-1878).

Editors note: This large cemetery is well cared for and is still a current burial ground in 2007.

Chapter II

William Susan Ikard
Son of Dr. Milton L. Ikard

(1847-1934)

W. S. Ikard was born in 1847 in Noxubee County, Mississippi. He married Kate Lewis, daughter of Col. E. D. Lewis of Kentucky. They had eight children: Willie Susan (Billie, a daughter), Jennie Bell (Patsy), Kate May (Katherine), Elijah Lewis, Emma John (Don, a daughter) *who married Marvin Smith*, Mary Frankie, Lee Davis, and Sallie Lorene (Sadie). He served with Mason's Co., Texas Cavalry, C. S. A. He died in 1934 in Henrietta, Texas.

The Ikard Family in Texas

As written by W. S. Ikard, Henrietta, Texas January 26, 1932
for J. Evetts Haley

The negro slave, Bose Ikard, was born in June 1847, and I was born July 7, 1847. We were both born at Summerville, Noxbee County, Mississippi. My father left there when I was two years old. He had two Negro women and a Negro man and this boy Bose.

He moved to Louisiana and then moved eight miles north of Honey Grove in Texas when I was five years old. Our nearest neighbor at that time was Young Burgher. My father was Dr. M. Ikard.

He had only a few cattle, sheep, and horses. From Lamar County he moved to Parker County about 1855. He was one of the first settlers of that county and located nine miles west of Weatherford on Grindstone Creek, where he lived until about 1882.

While in Louisiana my father lived in Union Parish. He had never been sick in Mississippi, but there we all got chills and fever and looked like all of us were going to die.

He read up on this "water cure," got us back up, and he went horseback prospecting to Honey Grove. My mother got us loaded up in a hack, and she rode horseback right behind it all the way to Texas. We drove. When we came to a steep bank, she'd jump off and hold on to the back end of the hack to keep it from turning over.

The Negros and furniture were carried in the wagon. We played with the Negro boys all the time. After getting to Texas, my father sold one of these Negro women to Oliver Loving for a thousand dollars and he took his pay in cows and calves at the rate of six dollars for a cow and calf. Then he took these to Picketville in Stephen County, and my next-to-the-oldest brother, R. E. Ikard, took charge of the cattle.

When the war broke out, he and George Reynolds came down to Weatherford and volunteered and went to R. E. Sanders's, a Methodist preacher's, company, which became a part of Buford's Regiment, The Nineteenth Texas Cavalry.

Then my father let some neighbor by the name of Schoolcraft have the cattle to take care of, and he was to get the fourth calf and the tenth beef steer for looking after them. He took some of all my father's cattle until after the war and branded V Bar <u>V</u>. My father had branded and I.

At that time my father had a boy horse colt, a yearling, and John Turner, one of our neighbors, had a boy horse colt of the same age sired by the same stallion. Turner's colt got out, drifted off, and he couldn't find it.

In the spring when we turned our horses out to graze, they came around to some salt that he kept near his house, and he found this colt of ours which looked just like his, only it was branded an I.

He drove it in and my brother Robert saw it in his corral. He told Turner that he had my father's colt, but he replied that it was his. He branded a J with a bar under it right over my father's I.

My father went to see him and they agreed to arbitrate it. Each side brought in its witnesses, and a committee each man had agreed upon to hear the evidence was to decide the case.

The witnesses were heard, and when my mother was heard she told the committee, "If you'll turn that colt loose, and if it doesn't go straight home to the salt block and go to licking salt, then Mr. Turner can have it." They turned him out and it did exactly as she said.

So my father changed the J Bar <u>J</u> into a V Bar <u>V</u> and started this as his own brand. Turner, by the way, was a preacher, and I have heard him preach many a time.   -W.S. Ikard-

William S. Ikard
Texas Heritage Hall of Honor
Inducted September 24, 2004
The Adolphus Hotel
Dallas, Texas

W.S. "Sude" Ikard of Henrietta is credited with bringing the first Hereford cattle to Texas in 1876. By doing so, he changed the Texas beef industry forever.

Sued Ikard got into the cattle business in 1865. He and his brother began rounding up cattle that had strayed south during the winter. They built their own herd by returning the strayed cattle to their owners and collecting a dollar a head, payable in cash or cattle. By 1867, the brothers were trailing their own cattle to Kansas City as often as three times a year, and on one of these drive Ikard passed through the Wichita Falls area which greatly impressed him.

Through various business ventures, he built his range in this area to 187,000 acres. He saw his first Herefords at the Philadelphia Centennial Exposition. Convinced that this breed would be adaptable to southwestern conditions, he shipped ten head by rail to Denison. Within a few decades, the sturdy, white-faced cattle dominated the Texas range.

Ikard was a founder of the Cattle Raisers Association of Texas. He also helped to organize it and served as the first president of the Texas Hereford Association. He remained active in the association until his death in 1934.

Editor's note: This was the printed program of the induction ceremony.

Chapter III

Ikard Smith and his wife Ann

Ikard Smith
(1919 — 2006)

Ikard Smith married Ann Myers in Wichita Falls in 1947. They had four children as follows: Cinda, Bryant, Clay and Cling. Wichita Falls has been their home through many endeavors. They have always supported it and it has supported them. Ikard died in 2006 and Ann still lives in their Wichita Falls home. Before his death, in fact all of his life, Ikard was involved in local Civic Endeavors and did much volunteer work.

Ikard Smith

By Mary Kemp

Ikard Smith came into this world in 1919 and made this world a better place. His father was Marvin Smith and his mother was Emma John Ikard, actually called "Don." His grandfather was William Susan (Sude) Ikard and his great grandparents were Dr. Milton L. Ikard and Isabella Tubb Ikard.

Most of Ikard's knowledge of the Ikard families, including the famous cowboy Bose Ikard, can be found in Section I of this book, entitled "The Real Lonesome Dove."

Ikard was always interested in the history of his family, but became very excited about his past when Larry McMurtry published *Lonesome Dove* in 1985.

You can be sure anything Ikard Smith says is the truth. We appreciate his family giving Nebo Valley Press the right to publish his history. From the day I asked him on the phone if he was a black Ikard or a white Ikard, both he and Ann have been my special friends.

Ikard Smith
Honors & Public Recognitions

Photo/Ben Noey Jr.

Ikard Smith poses with a painting of his great-grandfather, Dr. Milton Ikard.

The above picture was published, with an excellent article,
in the *Wichita Falls Times and Record* shortly after Ikard Smith learned
that Bose Ikard was a fictional character in the Lonesome Dove book.

In the article much was discussed about the *Lonesome Dove*
book, but one statement of Ikard's, as far as is known, was never printed
elsewhere. It is as follows:

"Rumor has it that Bose killed a soldier while protecting a lady's
honor. Bose had to leave the area or be hanged. My grandfather, Dr.
Milton Ikard, wrote him a letter of introduction and sent him to work for
Charles Goodnight." All Ikards seem to feel this was another side of
Bose's nature, to protect anyone, especially a "Lady".

"For his self less public service pursued with integrity"
City Magazine Names Ikard Smith Citizen of the Year
Wichita Falls, Texas
1988

It was spring, but the cold winds of change wrought by federally ordered desegregations were just reaching gale force.

Chilling differences bitterly divided the Wichita Falls school board that spring of 1970, and the debates centered on Wichita Falls' effort to pursue desegregation with deliberate speed. For several years, the board had grappled with the problem — ever since the federal Office of Civil Rights informed the district in early February 1968 of its intention to review the district's compliance with federal law. School Board President Ikard Smith, who has been on the board eight years, tried to set the tone when he issued a statement in reaction to the Office of Civil Rights announcement:

"We are confident that this community can, by united action, solve any problem to the satisfaction of our citizens and the Department of Civil Rights. Our prime concern is that every student in Wichita Falls has the best educational opportunity regardless of race, color or location of residence."

But the action was not to be united, and in the spring of 1970, as Smith was serving his fourth year as board president and his 10th year as a member, the winds of change turned into a blue northern that swept Smith out of office.

In late April, Smith resigned from the board a day after a majority of trustees voted to fire the superintendent of schools, who himself had overseen a desegregation plan. In retrospect, Smith recalls that the issue then was relatively simple to define: He felt the question facing the board was how to desegregate, not whether the schools should be desecrated. Others on the board disagreed. They were not yet willing to desegregate.

The situation presented Smith with a dilemma he had not yet faced before in his long parallel career of public service: to stay or to quit in the interest of doing the right thing, He left and in doing so made a statement about the conduct of public affairs that was more of a service than he could have performed by remaining on the board.

It is this kind of selfless public service that has prompted *City Magazine* to name Ikard Smith as Citizen of the Year for 1988. But it is only one example of many that can be cited when reflection on Smith's lifetime of devotion to his hometown, both as a merchant as a community leader.

For 40 years, few community endeavors have been achieved without his leadership and support. He has been in the forefront of support for the Wichita Falls Symphony Orchestra, the Wichita Falls Museum and Art Center, Board of Commerce & Industry, United Way, the YMCA, the March of Dimes, the industrial foundation, Boy Scouts of America, West Texas Chamber of Commerce, Woman's Forum, Midtown Now Inc. and Floral Heights United Methodist Church.

In addition to his ten years on the school board, he has been on the board of the Wichita County chapter of American Red Cross, advisory committees for city government and was a regent for Midwestern State University.

"I'd say he is characterized by three tings," said *City Magazine* publisher James D. Lonergan in announcing Smith's selection. "First, he really deeply cares about people and the city. Second, he has demonstrated that doing the right thing, even if it costs you a friendship, is what should be done, and third, he is wiling to assume responsibility. I have never seen anyone more willing to volunteer."

Beyond that, Smith ahs been chosen as an example of the kind of leadership Wichita Falls must continue to have if it is to thrive and grow in the future. "Who," Lonergan asked, "is coming behind him?"

Others in the community cited other places he could settle down after the war ended. Instead, he decided to return to Wichita Falls to go into business with his father.

"I didn't want to leave town," he said. "I thought I could make this thing work. At the time my father appeared elderly, and in four years he had a stroke. My daddy had been here all his life, and I thought that's what I was supposed to do."

By 1950, Smith was chief executive officer of McClurkans, and even though the business was sold in 1982, he is still senior chairman of the board. He said following in his parents' footsteps and his desire to help were the reasons for his civic involvement.

"I guess you just like a town, and if you can help a little, why not?" he said.

Besides that, he said, keeping active keeps you young. (Smith's 25 years of early morning jogging has also helped him stay young.) And he enjoys helping, even when he doesn't truly get a lot out of it. For example, he has been a major help to the Wichita Falls Symphony, yet he admits he is tone deaf.

"It gives me some self-satisfaction that I've helped a little," he said. Smith went on to say he believes that having a symphony and a museum makes "this a better city, a better place to raise children. We should keep making this town a better place to live."

While he has been active in many things, Smith said his greatest satisfaction has come from his work with public education.

"When you can help others, that's the great feeling that comes back: the bond issues, growth and improvement of our educational system."

Smith said he isn't afraid economic downturns will make the city any less a good place to be. He puts his actions where his mouth is. Just last year, he agreed to head a $3 million campaign to provide an endowment for and expansion of the museum and art center. His acceptance of the chairmanship of the fiver-year drive, which was launched as the price of oil dropped precipitously, is typical.

"This is my town," he said, "and I want to see it grow."

Smith is ever the optimist. "We've got a great university, we've got a good service town; I can think of a lot of good reasons to live here. I feel happy about my life here, and of course I will continue to stay and do what I can to make it a better town."

This article, written by Carroll Wilson, was printed in City Magazine.

The Saga of Bose Ikard

Come let me tell a story of a cowboy of great fame. He came to
Texas as a slave and took his master's name.
When freedom came he chose to stay close to the ones who
cared. They taught him how to rope the broncs and ride them if he
dared.

While riding with the Ikard herds, he met the Loving crew. He
gained more friends who did not care that he was black — it's true.
He sang the songs his mammy sang. He hummed them soft and
low. The cattle quieted by his voice. He rode round to and fro.

Soon drives were started to the North, and Loving had a plan;
to join Goodnight and then go west. That's how the route began.
They trusted Bose about all men. He was a faithful hand. They
often gave their funds to him, as they neared outlaw land.

Though Bose was black and Goodnight white, their friendship
formed and grew. And when the drives would finally end, it lasted
strong and true. When Bose returned to Weatherford, Goodnight
would visit there. They'd laugh about the good old days,
'till death would part the pair.

They placed Bose in a special spot. But no one ever dreamed
that crowds would flock to view his grave; that he would be esteemed.
McMurtry pictured him so well. In his tale *The Lonesome
Dove*, he became a symbol of cooperative love.

Old Bose would not know how to act, were he to come today.
For he just loved to drive the herds along the lonely way.
He sang the songs his mammy sang. He hummed them soft and
low. The cattle quieted by his voice. He rode round to and fro.

By Ruth E. Reuther   *Poet Laureate of Texas, 1987-88*
Prepared after a talk by Ikard wherein he reported true facts.
*Editor: Ikard Smith was very proud of this poem when he presented to
Mary Kemp for historical purposes.*

Chapter IV
Bose Ikard
(1843-1929)

(This is the story written by Mary Kemp that was approved by the Texas Historical Commission in 1990 and thus came the Texas Historical Marker that now stands at his grave in Old City Greenwood Cemetery, Weatherford, Texas, along with the Special Marker Charles Goodnight placed there in 1929. The Texas Historical Marker has the correct birth and death date for Bose as proven by Census Records.)

Bose Ikard

Bose Ikard, later known as the "Black Cowboy" who blazed the Goodnight-Loving Trail on numerous cattle drives from 1866 to 1871, was born in Mississippi in July 1843. (1)

He came to Texas with his master, Dr. Milton L. Ikard, when he was but a small child. Dr. Ikard came to Texas in 1852 and settled in southwest Parker County in 1855.

Bose Ikard's wife, Angeline Ikard, was born 19 August 1853 somewhere in Texas, and died 29 May 1902 in Parker County. She is buried in the same cemetery as Bose, but not beside him, that cemetery being the Old City Greenwood Cemetery on the north side of Weatherford. (2)

Bose and Angeline were the parents of: Benjamin, B–1869, who married Henrietta Hutchison 1 March 1987; Samuel, B–1875; Indiana, B–1881; Ester H., B–1884 and died 1885; Leaven Maude, B–1888; Isabell, B–1891, and they were all born in Texas. It is believed they were all born in Weatherford, Texas. Ester H. is buried in Old City Greenwood Cemetery near her mother Angeline and other relatives. (3)

One of the most famous cattle drives recorded in history is the Goodnight-Loving Cattle drive from Texas to New Mexico and Colorado. Their first cattle drive was a success in 1866 and Bose Ikard was with them.

The second cattle drive in 1867 is the most publicized as it was the one Oliver Loving lost his life from wounds he received in a battle with the Indians near Eddy, New Mexico.

Loving and one drover had gone on ahead of Goodnight, Ikard and the cattle when the two were attacked. Loving lived long enough for Goodnight to catch up and it was at Lovings's request Goodnight returned to New Mexico and returned his body for burial in Weatherford, Texas in January 1868.

Loving died 26 September 1867. The place where Loving was wounded is now known as Loving's Bluff. Loving's widow lived in Weatherford until her death in 1884 and is buried beside the now famous Loving. A Texas Historical Marker and a Republic of Texas Marker now marks his burial place. (4)

Charles Goodnight went on other cattle drives and was accompanied by Bose Ikard. But it was not the same without Loving. In 1871, Goodnight married Miss Mary Ann Dryer, a Weatherford school teacher. The couple moved to the Palo Duro Canyon area. He died when he was 95 and is buried in Goodnight, Texas. (5)

Charles Goodnight and Oliver Loving have been written about many times, and each time a reference is made to the faithful black cowboy, Bose Ikard.

However, since the fictional book entitled *Lonesome Dove*, they have become even more famous and so has Bose Ikard. In the movie, Bose, is depicted as "Deets" and plays an important role in the trail drive. However, he is killed early in the movie and that is the "fiction" part. Bose was not harmed and after more cattle drives with Goodnight, he returned to Weatherford to live the remainder of his life. (6)

BOSE AND ANGELINE IKARD'S CHILDREN

Although we know they had six children born between 1869 and 1891, nothing is known of any of them except Benjamin, the oldest. He was born in 1869 somewhere between the 1867 cattle drive and other cattle drives Bose made with Goodnight before Goodnight quit the cattle drives in 1871.

Benjamin Ikard married Henrietta Hutchison 1 March 1897 and they had four children. Their sons were Hugh, Frank, Charlie and the youngest child was a daughter named Cleon. She was born 11 May 1899 in Weatherford, Texas. She married Mitchell Rucker 24 January 1917 in Weatherford, where Mitchell lives today (1989) at the age of 90.

Mitchell was the son of Benjamin Rucker and Leona Pickard Rucker and the grandson of Willis and Cynthia Moore Pickard. Willis Pickard came here as a slave with the A. L. Pickard family who settled in the Spring Creek Community in southern Parker County in 1856.

Mitchell and Cleon had four daughters born to them in Parker County before Cleon's death 11 December 1936. They are: Mary Mitchette George, Florine Gwendolyn Roddy, Cleo Fran McQueen and Edna Jane Hopkins.

Mitchette died in 1969 and Jane lives in California. Cleo and Florine both still reside in Weatherford and are responsible for much of the data in this story. They are great-granddaughters of Bose and Angeline Ikard.

Neither Cleo nor Florine can really remember their great grandfather Bose Ikard or his burial in 1929. Cleo who would have been around seven years of age seems to recall what he looked like. Florine, a little older than Cleo, just does not remember. (7)

DR. MILTON L. IKARD, Bose Ikard's master, was born in Tennessee in 1812 and came with his wife and five sons to Texas in 1852 and on to Parker County in 1855 and settled nine miles southwest of Weatherford. From 1855 to 1875, Dr. Ikard was engaged in the cattle and farming business with his sons.

Together they fought many battles with the Indians in order to survive before the Indian raids stopped in Parker County in the late 1870s. The Ikard boys went on to become big cattlemen in several Texas counties.

Dr. Ikard seemed to be successful in all his endeavors and was elected to the 15th Legislature in 1876 where he represented the 15th District of Texas, including Parker County. In addition to farming and ranching through the years, he provided for his family through the professions of Hydropathic Doctor, Proprietary Medicine, and as a School Teacher.

Dr. Ikard married Isabella Tubbs on 17 March 1847. Isabella was born in 1812 in Tennessee and died in Parker County in 1881.

Dr. Ikard died in Parker County in 1882 and he and Isabella are buried in the old Cox Cemetery near their old home place in present Millsap area. (8 & 9)

At the end of the Civil War in 1865 Bose Ikard became a free man. History relates that he stayed on as an employee of Dr. Ikard until 1866 when he went on the first cattle drive with Charles Goodnight, the man who was to become a life long friend.

It is said, but we have no proof, that Bose returned to New Mexico with Goodnight to bring back Loving's body in the fall of 1867. Goodnight relied on Ikard for so much during those years that it would seem he probably did go back a long with the others.

Apparently, Bose Ikard, returned to Weatherford for good around 1871. He already had one child born in 1869 and the next was born in 1875. This is all we have to go on.

Bose Ikard died on Friday 4 January 1929 in Austin, Texas where he had been with a sister for a short time. His body was shipped by train to Weatherford arriving on Sunday. Funeral services and burial took place Monday afternoon at City Greenwood Cemetery.

The Daily Herald, Weatherford, Texas dated 7 January 1929 reports: "Bose Ikard was well known to nearly all of the older residents of Weatherford where he lived perhaps 50 years. He was very old at the time of his death being variously guessed from 85 to 90, by those who knew him. He had been living in Austin but a short time." (10)

Actually, we now know, Bose was born in July 1843 in Mississippi so he would have been 85 years old when he died in January 1929. Bose Ikard's age has been incorrectly reported in the past as having been born in 1847 or 1853. Charles Goodnight was guessing when he later had a grave marker for him and others were saying 1847 as he was guessed to be five years old when he came to Texas in 1852 with Dr. Ikard. The 1880 and 1890 Parker County Census verify his birth date July 1843.

In May 1929, Charles Goodnight, living in Claredon, Texas, heard of his old friend, Bose Ikard's death. He wrote his niece's husband, Mr. T. W. Stanley, Superintendent of Weatherford schools, to see about getting marker for Bose and he would pay for same. This he stated he wanted to do for his old cowboy friend.

On 17 May 1929, Mr. Goodnight answered a correspondence from Mr. Stanley wherein Goodnight approved the marker and inscription and sent a check to cover same.

In the letter Goodnight stated: "I've always felt under great obligation to old Bose and he was a real friend to me. We went through some terrible trials during those four years on the trail. While I had a good constitution and endurance, after being in the saddle for several days and nights at a time on various occasions, and I'd find I could not stand it any longer, I would ask Bose if he would take my place. He never failed to answer me in the most cheerful and willing manner and strange to say was the most skilled and trusted man I had. If I can see my way to do it, will the grounds stand form setting a few cedars around the grave?" (11)

On 18 May 1929, Weatherford Marble and Granite Works, through its owner, Alex Rawlins, installed one Winnsboro Granite marker at City Greenwood Cemetery for the sum of $60 paid by Charles

Goodnight. Weatherford Marble and Granite Works is now Alex Rawlins and Sons Monuments and the original letter and invoices were loaned to us by Nancy Deison, great granddaughter of Alex Rawlins who made the stone in 1929. (12)

The grave stone reads:

Bose Ikard – 1859 – 1928

Served with me four years on the Goodnight-Loving trail, never shirked a duty or disobeyed an order, rode with me in many stampedes, participated in three engagements with Comanches, Splendid behavior.

C. Goodnight.

Of course we now know that Bose was born in 1843 and died in 1929 and that Goodnight was just guessing at the age, but he was not guessing at his feelings for Bose Ikard. At any rate, Goodnight's installing the marker for his old friend was well received by his family, friends, and the news media.

In Weatherford today, the Parker County Historical Commission receives as many request for directions to Bose Ikard's grave as we do for directions to Oliver Loving's grave. The movie *Lonesome Dove* is responsible for many tourists asking to visit these two graves, located in the same cemetery, only a scant distance apart.

The 1978 GREAT AMERICAN NEGRO CALENDAR featured Bose Ikard as "The Cowboy who blazed the Goodnight-Loving Trail" in 1867 when Loving was killed.

The calendar depicts Bose as a good bronc rider and exceptional nighthawk and took well to the rugged life of a drover. They quote Goodnight, "He was so trustworthy that he always gave Bose his bankroll to carry on the trail." Also Goodnight is quoted, "Bose surpassed all my hands in endurance, stamina and fighting ability and he was my detective, banker and everything else in Colorado, New Mexico and the other wild country I was in. When we carried money, I gave it to Bose. I have trusted him farther than any living man."

In 1889, it is reported that Bose considered homesteading in Colorado but Goodnight persuaded him to remain in Texas where he became a farmer and laborer. The two men remained good friends to the end. (13)

When Bose Ikard was born into slavery in 1843 his birth was probably not even recorded. Whether he was born into the Ikard (white) family and took their name or whether Dr. M. L. Ikard purchased him later is not known.

We only know he came to Parker County in 1855 as a small slave boy and worked as a slave for the Ikard family until after the Civil War. At the time, he blazed the Goodnight-Loving trails with 2,000 head of cattle, he was truly an unusual black man.

He died in 1929 with a scant write up in the local paper. But as everyone became interested in their roots and in past history of our county and our state, Bose Ikard, along with Charles Goodnight and Oliver Loving became heroes of the early cattle drive history. All of the descendants of Bose Ikard have been well-respected citizens of the City of Weatherford and the County of Parker.

****

We the Family of Bose Ikard and We the Parker County Historical Commission are proud to count Bose Ikard as an important part of our past history and do hereby ask that a historical marker be granted to be placed at this grave to not only commemorate his past but to correct the information on his present tombstone.

Submitted by:

Mary Kemp, Secretary Treasurer Parker County Historical Commission and the Great

Granddaughters of Bose Ikard, Florine Roddy and Cleo McQueen.

Court House, Weatherford, Texas
1886

This 1886 Court House picture was used by the Parker County Historical Commission for the exterior restoration of the Courthouse started in 1986.

Bose Ikard (1843-1929)
Works Cited

1. 1880 Census of Parker County
2. 1900 Census of Parker
3. Grave Markers in Old City Greenwood Cemetery
4. Double Log Cabin, by G. A. Holland 1937, pp. 78-82
5. Double Log Cabin, by G. A. Holland 1937, pp. 78-82
6. Lonesome Dove, by Larry McMurty, made into a movie in 1989
7. History of Parker County 1980,
    by the Parker County Historical Commission, p. 526
8. Lineage and History of Dr. Milton L. Ikard and his sons, compiled by Mrs. Lynn Boyd
    [Edwina Ikard, great granddaughter of Dr. Ikard (1966)]
9. Historical Sketch of Parker County, by Smythe 1877, p. 382
10. Weatherford Daily Herald, 7 January 1929
11. Letter from Charles Goodnight to T. W. Stanley on 17 May 1929
12. Weatherford Marble and Granite Works, Weatherford, Texas –contract for grave marker for Bose Ikard
13. 1978 The Great American Negro Calendar –
    featuring Bose Ikard as "Black Cowboy"

Other Works

- Old City Greenwood Cemetery Records
- Current Pictures of Burials at Cemetery
- *The Weatherford Democrat*, Sunday 16 October 1966, Ikard (White) Reunion
- *The Weatherford Democrat*, 14 November 1983, "On The Trail of Bose Ikard, Early Day Cowboy," by Mike Bedwell
- *The Weatherford Democrat*, 17 October 1982, "Oliver Loving's Last Ride Ended Here at Greenwood Cemetery," by Mike Bedwell
- Conversations with Florine Roddy and Cleo McQueen, great granddaughters of Bose Ikard – Weatherford residents.
- Old City Directory of Weatherford, Texas 1907
- *The Daily Herald*, 8 June 1929, Story of Goodnight Installing Bose Ikard Marker
- *The Weatherford Democrat*, 8 June 1929, Story of Goodnight Installing Bose Ikard Marker

Texas Historical Marker Inscription
Bose Ikard
(July 1843-January 4, 1929)

Born a slave in Mississippi, Bose Ikard came to Texas as a child with the family of his owner, Dr. Milton L. Ikard. He remained as an employee of Dr. Ikard following his emancipation, but in 1866 joined a cattle drive to Colorado led by Charles Goodnight and Oliver Loving. Ikard became one of Goodnight's best cowboys and a trusted friend. Following his work in the cattle drives, Ikard settled in Weatherford. He and his wife Angeline were the parents of six children. When he died in 1929 at age 85, Goodnight had a granite marker erected at his Grave.

****

This is the granite headstone Charles Goodnight commissioned for Bose Ikard's grave

Texas Historical Commission article March 1991
Printed by *The Medallion*, the Commission's publication

For more than 60 years, a small headstone has marked the final resting place of black cowboy Bose Ikard, best known as the trusted friend of Charles Goodnight, legendary Texas rancher and trailblazer. The headstone, commissioned by Goodnight, reads:

Served with me four years on the Goodnight-Loving trail, never shirked a duty or disobeyed an order, rode with me in many stampedes, participated in three engagements with Camanches, splendid behavior. C. Goodnight.

Despite his close ties to Goodnight, for years little was known about Ikard, who was buried in Weatherford in 1929 at the age of 85. Much has been written about the long and colorful life of Goodnight, who went onto become a renowned Texas rancher, and Oliver Loving, who died of gangrene poisoning after being wounded in a skirmish with Indians on the trail in 1867.

Ikard, however, all but faded into obscurity – until 1985, that is, when Larry McMurtry's popular novel Lonesome Dove was published, rekindling an interest in the famous Goodnight-Loving trail and the men associated with it.

Although McMurtry's main characters are fictional, they are based loosely on Goodnight, Loving and Ikard. The book sparked so much interests in Ikard, local historian Mary Kemp decided to research his life. Her efforts resulted in the dedication of a historical marker at Ikard's grave last October.

Born in Mississippi in 1843, Bose Ikard came to Parker County in the 1850s as a young slave to the Dr. M. L. Ikard family. One year after the Civil War ended, in 1866, Ikard signed on with Goodnight's first cattle drive, which snaked its way from Texas to New Mexico and Colorado. During the drive Ikard proved to be one of Goodnight's best cowboys, and Goodnight soon came to depend on his varied skills.

"He was my detective, banker and everything else in Colorado, New Mexico and other wild country I was in," Goodnight once said. "When we carried money, I gave it to Bose. I have trusted him farther than any living man."

Encouraged by the success of the first cattle drive, Goodnight and Loving embarked on a second drive in 1867. It was during this expedition that Loving died at what is now known as Loving's Bluff, near Eddy, New Mexico. Goodnight accompanied his partner's body back to Weatherford for burial, but it is not certain whether Ikard joined him. What is certain is that Goodnight's taste for cattle drives diminished after Loving's death, and although Ikard accompanied him on several more, the two men ended their expeditions in 1871. Goodnight married Mary Ann Dryer, a Weatherford teacher, and moved to Palo Duro Canyon. Ikard settled down to a quiet life as a farmer and laborer. He and his wife, Angeline, were the parents of six children.

Years later, when Goodnight heard of Ikard's death, he commissioned the granite headstone for his old friend and cattle drive companion. Already in his 90s, Goodnight was but a few months from death himself. In a letter to his niece's husband, T.W. Stanley, who was coordinating placement of the headstone in Weatherford, Goodnight expressed his sentiments: "I've always felt under great obligation to old Bose and he was a real friend to me. We went through some terrible trails during those four years on the trail While I had a good constitution and endurance, after being in the saddle for several days and nights at a time on various occasions and I'd find I could not stand it any longer, I would ask Bose if her would take my place. He never failed to answer me to in the most cheerful and willing manner and strange to say was the most skilled and trusted man I had."

****

One Hundred Year Old Saddle

R.T. Frazier Saddle was ordered by W.W. (Bill) Tanner, while he worked at the XIT Ranch in 1907. This saddle has been in the Panhandle Museum for over 30 years. This year, 2007, it will be moved to the Doss Museum in Weatherford, Texas. The Tanner Family settled in Weatherford in 1890.

Dedication of Bose Ikard's Gravesite Historical Marker

Weatherford Democrat photo by Barbara Lombardi — Oct. 18, 1990

Ikard Smith, great grandson of Dr. Milton L. Ikard, standing next to Florine Roddy, great granddaughter of Bose Ikard, delivers the dedication address of the Texas Historical Commission's gravesite marker for Bose Ikard. Smith referred to Bose in the words of his own early ancestor — a most "trustworthy man."

Bose Ikard historical marker

Pioneers Remembered with Markers

By Carolyne Gould

as published in the *Fort Worth Star-Telegram*, October 1990

Fort Worth Star-Telegram/ Joyce Marshall

Descendents of Bose Ikard, who came to Texas as a slave, stand near the Texas historical marker at his grave in Weatherford.

WEATHERFORD – Most of the people gathering yesterday to honor Bose Ikard, their cowboy ancestor who helped lead the great Texas cattle drives, knew him only from stories.

But Melvin George of Weatherford once met Ikard, and though George was only about 7 years old, the memory is still vivid.

"He was the first cowboy I ever saw," George said. "He was standing on a porch wearing a big cowboy hat, boots, Levi's and a big buckle on his belt. He took a quarter out of his pocket, and with a flick of his finger and thumb, tossed it to me. Boy do I wish I'd kept it."

George, 72, later married one of Ikard's great-granddaughters. He was at the ceremony yesterday with about 200 others to honor the cowboy and two other pioneers of the area.

The group included relative and friends from as far away as Anchorage, Alaska. They witnessed the dedication of a Texas historical marker at Ikard's grave in Old City Greenwood Cemetery in Weatherford, and state historical grave markers at the graves of G. A. Holland and J. R. Couts.

Holland, who lived form 1859 to 1946, settled in Poolville. He was a teacher, postmaster, justice of the peace, county tax collector, banker and Weatherford mayor. Couts (1833-1904) came to Parker County after the Civil War and became a successful banker and influential citizen.

Ikard was born a slave in Mississippi in 1843 and was brought to Weatherford in 1852 by his owner, Dr. Milton Ikard. After emancipation, he joined a cattle drive to Colorado, riding with Charles Goodnight and Oliver Loving to blaze the Goodnight-Loving trail. Ikard, who settled in Weatherford after the cattle drives, died in 1929. He is buried a few yards from his friend and trail companion, Oliver Loving.

About 100 descendants of Bose Ikard and Dr. Ikard attended the ceremony honoring the man Charles Goodnight called his "detective, banker and everything else."

Ikard is believed to be the model for the black cowboy Deets in Larry McMurtry's cattle-drive epic *Lonesome Dove.*

Six of Bose Ikard's direct descendants of Bose Ikard and Dr. Ikard attended the dedication yesterday: great-granddaughters Cleo

McQueen of Weatherford and Florine Roddy of Fort Worth; great-grandsons Welton Woodfork Jr. of Dallas and Don George of Grand Prairie; great-great-great-granddaughter Kendra Roddy of Arlington; and great-great-grandson Leon Roddy of Arlington.

Descendants of Dr. Ikard also attended, including Mac McIlvain, who flew 5,000 miles for the weekend from Alaska. His brother, Jim McIlvain, came from San Jose, Calif.

Ikard Smith, the great-grandson of Dr. Ikard, brought a message from J. Evetts Haley, author of *Charles Goodnight, Cowman and Plainsman.*

Haley told Smith in August that he numbered Ikard amount the great cowboys of the West, who are remembered for their "trueness, bravery and hardihood. They kept their places around the herd…always ready…a timid man not amoung them. I salute him."

Leon Roddy, a policeman and minister, offered the dedication prayer, saying the group was there to "pay honor to Mr. Holland, Mr. Couts and Bose Ikard. Let their lives be an inspiration to us."

(Editor-The Texas Historical Markers for G. A. Holland and J. R. Couts were dedicated the same day. An estimated 200 people attended the Bose Ikard ceremony.)

The Great American Negro Calendar
1978

Bose Ikard had a complete page of stories and drawings concerning his cowboy history as early as 1978 in the above-mentioned calendar.

There was no real picture of him and a drawing was used. This drawing was all anyone had of Bose until after the Texas Historical Marker Dedication at the Old City Greenwood Cemetery in October 1990.

Shortly after the dedication, a great granddaughter of Bose, Jane Rucker Hopkins from California, notified Cleo Rucker McQueen, her sister in Weatherford, Texas, that she had found some old photos in their Aunt Maude's trunk in California. Aunt Maude had died in 1974 in California. Now how to get them to Weatherford?

Cleo McQueen's son, Welton Woodfork Jr., decided to visit his brother, Harry Earl McQueen and Aunt Jane Hopkins in California — and here came the great pictures. Cleo placed them in the hands of Mary Kemp, and they hung in Kemp's Texas Butane Company in Weatherford for many years.

Visitors from all over came to view them and take pictures. They were shown on the television shown "The Eyes of Texas" in a 30-minute segment, which include Cloe Smith of Garner, the Abandoned Cemetery Association, Mary Martin.

Later Kemp and McQueen released the pictures to a new Weatherford elementary school opened in 2002 named in Bose Ikard's honor. The pictures remain in Bose Ikard Elementary School to this day.

144

Bose Ikard Family Pictures

Angeline Ikard
Wife of Bose Ikard

Maude Ikard
Daughter of Bose Ikard

Indiana Ikard
Daughter of Bose Ikard

Cleon Ikard
Daughter of Ben Ikard
Granddaughter of Bose Ikard
with husband Mitchell Rucker
in Weatherford, Texas

Weatherford Public Library's Heritage Gallery
Loving-Goodnight and Ikard exhibit
Grand Opening October 3, 1994

The grand opening of the Weatherford Public Library's new Heritage Gallery, held Oct. 3, 1994, introduced the soon to open "Loving–Goodnight, Ikard Trail Drivers" exhibit. The event, celebrated with a Weatherford Chamber of Commerce ribbon cutting, honored all three

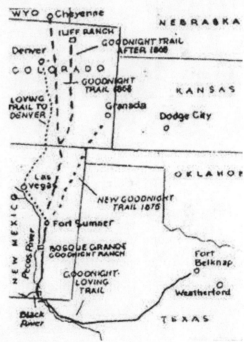

cowboys and their families.

This map of the Goodnight-Loving trail was displayed in the Weatherford Public Library Heritage Gallery's 1994 trail drivers exhibit.

Heritage Gallery Ribbon Cutting

This picture of the Weatherford Public Library's Heritage Gallery's grand opening, taken by Tina Jackson, ran in *The Weatherford Democrat's* Oct. 4, 1994 edition.

The photo's caption read: Descendants of Oliver Loving and Bose Ikard were joined by members of the Chamber of Commerce Ambassadors at the grand opening and ribbon cutting of the Heritage Gallery at the Weatherford Public Library. The gallery features an exhibit on trail drivers Loving, Goodnight and Ikard.

Bose Ikard Write Ups

The Negro Cowboys
by Philip Durham and Everett L. Jones
Published 1965

In chapter 7, entitled Lincoln County and Tombstone, of this book, Bose Ikard is cited for his acclaimed experience with Charles Goodnight and Oliver Loving. Durham and Jones highlight his fame as a great cowboy and his well-known trail driving ability.

Celebrating Black Cowboys
by E. Jackson, Jr.
Special for 1997 Black History Month

Bose Ikard was again recognized for his cowboy activities. A full page was devoted to Bose, along with Charles Goodnight, Oliver Loving and Lonesome Dove.
(Editor's note: E. Jackson Jr. was president and general manger of radio station MAJIC 102.)

Texas Trail of Fame
Fort Worth Stockyards 1997

The Fort Worth Star-Telegram's, Art Chapman, gave a detailed description of the historical event in October 1997 when Bose Ikard and others were inducted as "New Stars to shine on the Trail of Fame." Each person, whose "star" will shine forever, was listed in a bulletin from the event.

Parker County historian Mary Kemp, her daughter Judy V. White, Bose Ikard's great-granddaughter Cleo McQueen and Helen Eldrige — all of Weatherford — traveled together to the event.

"We were treated royally and enjoyed a great lunch with many of Bose's family members," Kemp said.

She said it was great to sit in the same company with the real Dale Evans. (Roy was sick at the time, but was also honored.)

Relatives and friends of Burk Burnettt, Amon G. Carter Sr., Charles Goodnight, John Justin Jr., Oliver Loving, Tad Lucas, Watt Matthews, Jose Navarro, Quanah Parker, Bill Pickett, Sid Richardson and Will Rogers also attended the event.

All of these people, along with Bose Ikard, already had a shining star or revealed it that day. Harry McQueen, son of Cleo McQueen and great-great grandson of Bose Ikard, made the trip from his California home, to accept the honor for the Ikard family. Harry McQueen has represented the Bose Ikard family on many occasions regarding trail drives and historical history.

Trail of Fame Star

This Star, featured in the Texas Trail of Fame, honors the famous black cowboy Bose Ikard in the Fort Worth Stockyards. It is a common stop for many tourists.

Oct. 26, 1997, *Fort Worth Star-Telegram* reporter, Karen Rouse, wrote an article entitled, "Legends of the West" picturing Loving, Ikard, Goodnight, Rogers, Matthews, R. Rogers and D. Evans.

Western Heritage Awards
National Cowboy Hall of Fame and Western Heritage Center
Oklahoma City — April 24, 1999

In 1999, the National Cowboy Hall of Fame inducted Bose Ikard into the Hall of Great Westerners. Kemper Marley of Phoenix, Arizona and John S. Justin Jr. of Fort Worth, Texas were also inducted at the ceremony. The Great Westerners Award is the highest honor the museum bestows. Bose Ikard joined Bass Reeves, Will Rogers, Teddy Roosevelt, Jess Chisholm, Willa Cather, and Sacagawea. Harry McQueen gave the acceptance speech.

Bose Ikard

Black Cowboys of Texas
Published by A&M University Press, College Station 2002

I refer to chapter 10, written by Bruce Shackleford about Bose Ikard, of the above book because I had the pleasure of assisting Mr. Shackleford in his presentation. There are 24 chapters about the black cowboys and girls of Texas, but I am the most grateful for chapter 10.

Since the research done at the time of Bose Ikard's historical marker dedication, it became clear both black and white Ikard's wanted to answer one question: Who was Bose Ikard's father?

All his history was pretty well recorded but this fact. Census records report 1843 as Bose Ikard's birth date and 1833 as his wife Angeline's birth date. They all agree, however, the slave records were not great in those days. Family members remember his mother's name as Rose King. His 1929 death certificate lists his father as Ikard and his mother as King.

Bruce Shackleford wrote in his story: "Bose Ikard's mother, named "King," was a slave owned by Dr. Milton L. Ikard, the owner of both Bose and his mother. Portraits of Bose Ikard and his owner Dr. Ikard reveal such a striking resemblance that even descendants of Dr. Ikard believe that Bose's father was the doctor. Charles Goodnight, a friend of the Ikard, was of the same belief."

What happened to Rose King? No one knows. But it seems to be the belief of relatives, both black and white, that Dr. Ikard was his father, and how we wish we knew what happened to Rose King.

Written by Mary Kemp

Bose Ikard Elementary School Dedication

Invitation reads:

We're building futures and opening doors in the Weatherford
ISD. Join us as we celebrate the opening of Bose Ikard Elementary.
Sunday, Sept. 8, 2002 — 2 p.m. at 100 Ikard Lane, Weatherford,
Texas.

Reception and Building Tour will follow the program.

Bose Ikard Elementary School

When Weatherford's Bose Ikard Elementary School opened in 2002, several parents did not recognize the name, said the school's principal Linda Starnes in a Feb. 18, 2004 article printed in *Weatherford/ Parker County Up Close* written by then special features writer Terry Evans.

However, many of Bose's descendants set everyone straight at the school's dedication. Bose Ikard, a Parker County resident for most of his life, was a slave brought to this area by Dr. Milton L. Ikard. His trail hand life was well documented for many years in many books. Though Martin Luther King Jr. is the focus of students nationwide, Ikard's contribution to Texas and Parker County warrants attention in Weatherford.

Starnes, who is still the school's principal in 2007, said she believes Bose Ikard would be proud of the school that carries his name.

Cleo McQueen, great granddaughter of Bose Ikard, attended the celebration with two of Ikard's great-great grandsons, Donald George of Grand Prairie and Welton Woodfork Jr. of Dallas.

Bill Shatford, the school district's assistant superintendent and chairman of the school naming committee, said the entire committee was intrigued by the idea of naming a school after a Texas hero who was a minority with local roots.

****

Mt. Pleasant School

The Mt. Pleasant School was the main educational facility for the community's black students from 1877 to 1954. It was called the Weatherford Colored School until 1936.

Bose Ikard descendants not only attended this school but one descendant, Florine Roddy, taught there for many years. She was teaching there when Weatherford schools integrated. I, Mary Kemp, was secretary, to Leonard Wilson the Weatherford school districts' superintendent, from 1944 to 1963. I was there when integration took place and when the actual meeting was held in the old Weatherford High School third floor study hall. I kept the school board minutes. It was a great time for all, very peaceful. I remember thinking, "This is a great historical time."

And it was. I remember the Gratts children along with Donald George, Leon Roddy, Welton Woodfork, Harry McQueen and many others who walked from Mt. Pleasant School to our office in the old high school on Alamo Street to pick up supplies, such as chalk, pencil sharpeners, books and more. They were a group of great kids and always welcome in our office.

In fact, a barracks type building was added to the Mt. Pleasant School, and was named "Wilson Hall" after my boss, Leonard Wilson. I understand that Wilson Hall has been torn down, but the old Mt. Pleasant School is sill there in a very sad state of repair. I wish it could be saved and granted a Texas Historical Marker.

Mt. Pleasant School 1921

****

Swan School

Another black school in Parker County's black history is connected to Oliver Loving as well. Weatherford resident, Helen Eldridge attended Swan School in Annetta, which was named for her great grandfather Lewis Swan. The land for the school was dedicated by Eldridge's ancestors, who were given the land after the second Good night-Loving trail blazing drive. Lewis and Nancy Swan were slaves of Oliver Loving, and it is believed that when Loving freed them, he gave them the land in Annetta. It was a one-room school — first through ninth grade.

The Annetta Community was a large community even before the 1900's. No picture of Swan School.

Also, there is a very important Black Cemetery in the area named DAWSON HACKETT and is on the list to be restored by the Abandoned Cemetery Assn. of Parker Co.

****

Chapter IV Sources
The Ikards

1. Black cowboys of Texas, Texas A&M University y—chapter 10 by Bruce Shackleford
2. Texas Historical Marker application as prepared by Mary Kemp—printed in its entirety
3. *Loving-Goodnight-Ikard Trail Drivers West* exhibit—Weatherford Library, 1994
4. Texas Trail of Fame—Fort Worth Stockyard, 1997
5. National Hall of Fame—Oklahoma City, Okla., 1999
6. The Negro Cowboys, by Philip Durham and Everett L. Jones, 1965
7. *Celebrating Black Cowboys*, by radio station MAJIC 102's special for Black History Month, 1997
8. *The Great American Negro Calendar*, 1978
9. "School's namesake cowboy was a Parker County hero"—*Weatherford/Parker County Up Close* by Terry Evans, 2004
10. Many articles written by Jon McConal—*Fort Worth Star-Telegram*
11. Many conversations with Cleo McQueen and family over the past 20 years. (Yes, we are both old now.)
12. Many articles in the *Weatherford Democrat, Fort Worth Star-Telegram* and other newspapers.
13. All sources already listed in back of the 1990 Texas Historical Marker dedication

(Editor's note: If I have missed someone or something, please forgive me as my memory does not begin to hang on as does the memory of Jack Borden, now 98 years old—but he will tell me what I missed. ~Mary Kemp)

Here ends the story of Bose Ikard

Of course there is more. However, if the life of Bose Ikard and his family was printed word for word from all records — this book would never be printed.

Thank you all for reading,
Nebo Valley Press
Leon Tanner, Mary Kemp

(Local Charities will benefit from the sale of this book)

Section V

Title Contest Entries

A committee was assembled to view the contest entries and it was a difficult job. Many wonderful entries were submitted in a very short time. Committee members were: Lois Johnson, Kaye Martino, Ann Saunders and Charlie Simmons.

The winning title was

Parker County Legends-Trail Bosses and Wild Hosses

Submitted by: Mary Bynum, Dennis, Texas

Thanks to Mary Bynum for several entries and for donating her contest money of $200.00 to the Abandoned Cemetery Association of Parker County, Inc.

Title Contest Entries

Louise Jones
　"The Lonesome Covey"
Wendy A. Bates
　" The Long Road Home"
Pat Cheng
　"The Promise of the Long Journey"
Kent Morgan
　" Brothers of the Prairie"
　"Partners 'Till the Sun Sets"
　" Comrades of the Saddle"
　" Friends 'Till the End of the Trail"
　"The Cattle Chasers"
　"Three Rode West"
Mary Pearson
　" Hammering Hoofs: The Trails of Weatherford
　　Cattleman: Goodnight- Ikard –Loving"
Toni Himes
　" Follow the Cloud
Martha McClung
　" Cattle Driving Legends: Charles Goodnight
　　Oliver Loving, Bose Ikard"
　" Pioneer Cattle Driving Trio: Charles
　　Goodnight, Oliver Loving, and Bose Ikard"
Jean Darter
　" Spurs and Saddles"
Faye Smith
　"Western Winds: The Story of Three Cowboys"

Donna Ware
  " A Trio of Trail Blazers: Parker County's
    Goodnight, Loving and Ikard"
  "A Trail Blazing Trio: Parker County's
    Goodnight, Loving and Ikard"
Linda Bagwell
  "Real True Grit: The Story of Three Cowboys
    and Indian-Fighters"
Tim Brown
  " Texas Pride, A Parker County Tribute"
Evelyn Payne
  "From_Weatherford to Lonesome Dove,
    The Real Story"
  "Trail Blazers: From Weatherford to Lonesome
    Dove"
  " Trail Blazers: The Men and Their Vision"
Girls at Euerka Dental Clinic
  "True Lonesome Heroes"
  "Ikard, The Lonesome Hero"
Mrs. Ona L. Weaver
  "Legend to Empty Saddles"

****

Thanks to all who entered the title contest!
Nebo Valley Press
South Parker County
Weatherford, Texas